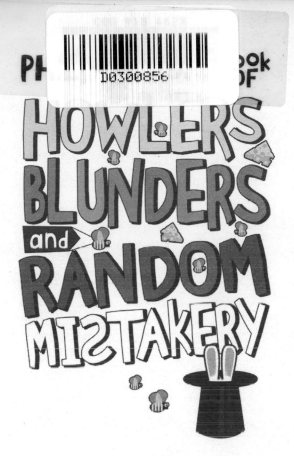

PHILIP ARDAGH'S BOOK OF

HOWLERS BLUNDERS and RANDOM MISTAKERY

Described as 'a national treasure' by the *Independent* and as 'one of life's fact-finders' by the *Scotsman*, Philip Ardagh has written books on subjects ranging from archaeology to space flight, and has still found time to write the bestselling Eddie Dickens children's novels, now translated into over thirty languages, to review children's books for the *Guardian* ('on a regularly irregular basis') and to appear at events and festivals around the world. He is married with one son.

Also by Philip Ardagh

Philip Ardagh's Book of
Absolutely Useless Lists
for Absolutely Every Day of the Year

PHILIP Ardagh's book OF HOWLERS BLUNDERS and RANDOM MISTAKERY

Illustrated by
Del Thorpe

MACMILLAN

First published 2009 by Macmillan Children's Books

This edition published 2010 by Macmillan Children's Books
a division of Macmillan Publishers Limited
20 New Wharf Road, London N1 9RR
Basingstoke and Oxford
Associated companies throughout the world
www.panmacmillan.com

ISBN 978-0-330-50807-0

1 3 5 7 9 8 6 4 2

A CIP catalogue record for this book is available from
the British Library.

Printed and bound in the UK by CPI Mackays, Chatham ME5 8TD

A message from Philip Ardagh

Most, if not all, books contain mistakes of some kind or other: typing, grammatical, spelling, factual. If there's an opportunity to get something wrong in print, you can be pretty sure that someone somewhere has done it. Or will do it.

The great thing about this book is that it's SUPPOSED to be full of mistakes. It's all about mistakes . . . and, if I get something wrong along the way, I can always claim that I did it on purpose!

Having said that, teams of people have pored – and, yes, that should be 'pored' not 'poured', whatever you may think – over these pages, trying to make sure that I've behaved myself and got things right as much as possible.

My thanks to them, especially Rachael Petty (who – oops! – actually spells her name without a second 'a').

Any errors are mine.

Philip Ardagh
Tunbridge Wells

A killing joke

Paul Hubert of Bordeaux, France, was convicted of murder and sentenced to life imprisonment in 1863. After he had spent over twenty years alone in a cell, his case was reopened and he was found to have been a victim of a terrible miscarriage of justice. Hubert had been convicted of murdering – er – HIMSELF!*

* No wonder they couldn't find the body

Forewarned is forearmed

In 1973, a group of international scientists made some forecasts as to what would happen in the following one hundred years. Predictions included that in the year 2000 every home in the developed world would have a complete electronic newspaper . . . which, thanks to the Internet, ain't that far from the truth. The prediction for 2007 was a little less accurate though: people who lose a limb would be able to grow a new one.*

* Not just yet

Out of the jaws of victory

In September 1862, during the American Civil War,* Unionist General Ambrose Burnside ordered his men to cross the Antietam Creek using the 38-metre-long Rohrbach Bridge: a narrow stone bridge, only wide enough for two people to walk side by side. This meant crossing it was a slow – and very dangerous – business.

All the Confederates had to do was line up 350 sharpshooters on a nearby ridge and fire at them. Burnside's men were easy targets. Most of them were killed.

Tragically, if the general had been better prepared, he'd have discovered that there were plenty of places along the river where his troops could simply have waded across in shallow water.

* The American Civil War (1861–1865) was between the Confederates (Southern states which broke away from the US) and the Unionists, who wished to keep the states together**
** The Unionists won, which is why, today, we have the *United* States of America

Today, the bridge has been renamed Burnside's Bridge. And the general himself? He got promoted.

President Abraham Lincoln said of Burnside: 'Only he could wring spectacular defeat out of the jaws of victory.'

The email deadlier than the mail

Claire McDonald received emails containing sensitive military information from, among others, the US Pentagon and the UK's Ministry of Defence. One email outlined communication problems on British warships and another discussed New Zealand's defence strategy!

Claire received these important communications because her email address had been included in the mailing list by a member of the Royal Navy . . .

. . . the only problem being that she was schoolgirl!

She replied to the emails on a number of occasions to point out that, perhaps, she shouldn't be receiving them, but it was a while before the matter was sorted out. Her email address was on the list due to a typing error!

A knockout idea

The idea of the Marquis of Queensberry Rules of boxing, introduced in 1867, was to try to finally put a stop to the bare-knuckle fights that so often ended in free-for-all brawls. It was thought that rules, such as three-minute rounds and having to wear boxing gloves, would make the sport less tough and more respectable. To begin with, however, many boxing gloves were worn skintight and actually inflicted much more damage to the opponent's body. Or head.*

* There were also some INCREDIBLY LONG fights. In 1893, boxers Andy Bowen and Jack Burke famously slugged it out in the ring for 7 hours and 9 minutes, in an epic 110-round match in America. Even then, it ended in a draw!

Missing the (compass) point

On 27 August 1883, the volcanic island of Krakatoa erupted with the biggest explosion ever to reach human ears. People heard it over 2,000 miles away, and the blast was picked up on scientific equipment in Britain (right on the other side of the world). The eruption created a tidal wave over 30 metres high,* which killed 36,417 people and destroyed over 160 towns and villages on the islands of Java and Sumatra.

The dust thrown up by the volcano affected the world's weather for the next three years. Snow in Ohio, USA, fell yellow and green instead of the usual white, and Britain enjoyed the most extraordinarily colourful sunsets.

So dramatic were events on that fateful day in August 1883 that in 1969 they were turned into a film called *Krakatoa, East of Java*. The problem with the choice of title is that Krakatoa is, in truth, WEST of Java!

* Travelling at over 40 miles an hour

Artful blunders!

 In 2001, artist Damien Hirst assembled ashtrays, beer bottles and paint tins to make the gallery look like an artist's studio (to mark the launch of his exhibition Painting By Numbers). Unfortunately, a cleaner cleaned it all up before the launch. The objects were frantically fished out of the dustbins. Hirst himself said that the whole mix-up had been 'very funny'.

 In 2004, a cleaner at Tate Modern threw away a plastic bag of rubbish, unaware that it was part of an exhibition!

 In January 2006, a visitor to Cambridge's Fitzwilliam Museum tripped over his shoelace and down a flight of stairs, smashing a 300-year-old Qing vase into 113 pieces in the process. It took six months to put it back together again but, amazingly, it's now back on display!

 In 2006, mega-rich American Steve Wynn had just agreed to sell his Picasso picture *Le Rêve* (*The Dream*) for £74 million when he stumbled and stuck his elbow through the canvas, creating a five-centimetre tear. Not surprisingly, the sale didn't happen!

 In the 18th century, a curtain was hung in front of Leonardo da Vinci's wall painting *The Last Supper* to 'protect' it. In fact, when closed, the curtain trapped moisture, actually damaging the picture.*

At the 240th Royal Academy Summer Exhibition, in 2008, a 2.7-metre-tall 'ceramic totem' entitled *Christina*, by Costa Rican artist Tatiana Echeverri Fernandez, was accidentally smashed by a visitor who apparently 'lost her balance'.

---

* If that wasn't bad enough, every time the curtain was drawn open, it scratched the paintwork!!!

Hotting up

In 1814, a 24-metre-high pagoda* was erected in St James's park, lit up by a staggering 10,000 gas-jets to introduce the idea of this new form of lighting to the public. Sadly, the whole thing burned down when it was hit by a rocket from a firework display! Not the best way to calm people's fear about the safety of using gas lighting!

* A many-tiered tower, built to look like a Hindu or Buddhist temple

How nutty . . . or not!

A peanut isn't, in fact, a nut.* It is a member of the pea family.**

* Despite what the name suggests
** As *part* of the name might (possibly) suggest

Some meddling here and there

The Chinese hosts of the 2008 Olympics made the mistake of thinking that a little sleight of hand at the opening ceremony of the games would either pass unnoticed or, if found out, be considered no big deal. BAD MISTAKE.

Firstly it was discovered that the little girl singing at the ceremony was miming the words sung by a 'less attractive' child!!!

Next it was revealed that some of the fireworks shown on huge screens forming the shapes of footprints leading to the Bird's Nest stadium weren't real but computer-generated.

Then – yup – another big boo-boo: the authorities admitted that children from China's dominant Han population were used in the ceremony to represent children of all 56 ethnic groups that make up China's population . . . rather than their coming from the actual ethnic groups as they'd originally claimed!

Still, as far as their performance in the games

themselves went, they made few mistakes. China ended up at the top of the medals table (if you award more points for a gold medal than for silver or bronze). According to the US, however, they were top of the medal table, not China, even though they won fewer races.*

* Go figure!!

Ditch it!

The Royal Military Canal was built in the county of Kent as 28 miles of defence against Napoleon's forces should they land in England.* What remains a puzzle to this day is why any military brain would think that a short length of narrow canal would put off an enemy army who would have had to cross the sea to attack in the first place.

Not only that, the canal wasn't actually finished until 1809 (by which time Napoleon's navy had suffered a serious defeat at the Battle of Trafalgar and had no plans to invade).

* Hadrian's Wall and Offa's Dyke are the only defensive structures in the UK that are longer than this

Mooning, everyone!

A lunar* month is often described as being 28 days when, in reality, it is (on average) 29.5 days long. A lunar month is the period between one new moon and the next.

* Lunar comes from the Latin *luna*, meaning 'moon'**
** The term 'lunatic' (meaning a person who is mentally ill or very silly) gets its name from the old belief that changes in the moon's cycle caused people to go mad for a bit***
*** And don't forget werewolves – people who were said to turn into wolves during a full *moooooon*!

A battle of wits

Lieutenant-Colonel Oreste Pinto was a Dutch member of Allied Counter-Intelligence in the Second World War. He was convinced that Emile Boulanger, a man he'd met for routine questioning, was a German spy and not a Belgian farmer as he claimed to be. Pinto did all he could to catch Boulanger out.

Boulanger was put in a cell and, when he was asleep, smoke was blown under his door and soldiers shouted, '*Feuer!*' (the German for fire). Boulanger ignored the cries, except for rolling over, until someone shouted, 'Fire!' in French. Then he leaped up. Pinto's attempt to catch the man out – if he really was a German spy, that is – had failed.

On another occasion, Lieutenant-Colonel Pinto turned to one of his men during an interrogation of Boulanger and made arrangements, in German, for Boulanger to be shot by firing squad in an hour's time! Once again, Boulanger didn't react in any way to suggest that he'd understood a word. By now Pinto was beginning to doubt his own instincts. Had he made a mistake? Was Boulanger really just the Belgian farmer he claimed to be?

The following day, Boulanger was taken to Oreste Pinto's office. There Pinto signed some papers and told Boulanger that he was free to go. Boulanger sighed with relief and turned to leave . . .

. . . Only then did he realize his terrible blunder. Pinto had spoken to him IN GERMAN. His cover was blown.

I scream for something cooler!

If you really want to cool down on a hot day, it's a mistake to think that ice cream is the answer. Ice cream contains both sugar and carbohydrates, which are oxidized in your body, giving off heat. Yes, h-e-a-t as in hot stuff . . . as in making you WARMER, not cooler.*

* Though your brain may tell you otherwise. And never underestimate the power of the brain. (Even yours)

18

Heads you lose

When his wife Eva Peron* died in 1952, President Peron of Argentina ordered the Post Office to issue some stamps in her memory. Each stamp in the series had a portrait of Eva on it. All well and good so far, except that the president also issued orders that when the stamps were stamped with the postmark by the post office, the mark mustn't disfigure his late wife's face.

Because part of the reason for a postmark is to make sure that a used stamp isn't peeled off and used again, this presented the Argentinian Post Office with a problem. Should they carry out their president's wishes and risk losing money, or postmark the stamps as usual and risk the the president's anger?

Judging by the used Eva stamps in people's stamp collections today, a number of stamp stampers weren't too good with their aim, or – perish the thought – deliberately postmarked Eva's head slap-bang in the middle!

* The subject of the Tim Rice and Andrew Lloyd Webber musical *Evita*

19

Get it write!

 The rather superb palindrome – spelled the same forwards and backwards – 'Go hang a salami I'm a lasagna hog!' only works if you misspell 'lasagne'.

 In Philip Ardagh's series of children's books Unlikely Exploits, Smoky the cat not only changes into smoke (which was intentional) but also changes gender (which wasn't). He starts out as a tomcat in *The Fall of Fergal* and is a she by the end of *The Rise of the House of McNally*!*

 It's a common mistake to think that Lewis Carroll created the names Tweedledum and Tweedledee. Although they're characters in *Alice Through the Looking-Glass* (first published in 1871),** the names first appeared in a poem by John Byrom in the 18th century.

* Oh dear. That was me, wasn't it?
** As *Alice Through the Looking-Glass, and What Alice Found There*

Second to none

After Cromwell's death in 1658, England's commonwealth was at an end, and the British monarchy was reinstated. With King Charles II on the throne, a regiment of foot soldiers marched all the way from its headquarters at Coldstream* down to London. There they met with the king on Tower Hill.

As professional soldiers, these men had been loyal to Cromwell and the Commonwealth and now Charles II needed them to be loyal to him. He ordered them to symbolically lay down their weapons – to end their association with Cromwell – and to pick them up again as his newly named 'Second Regiment of Guards'.

This was a mistake.

They refused.

They were too proud to be referred to as the second anything! The king quickly realized the error of his ways so changed his orders.

* On the Scottish borders

'Coldstream Guards,' he commanded, 'pick up your arms.' This they did, and since then they have been known as the Coldstream Guards.

With their familiar red jackets and high bearskin hats, this is the regiment which, among other duties, guards Buckingham Palace to this day. Their motto is *Nulli Secundus*: second to none.

Right? No, doubly wrong!

One of Van Dyke's famous paintings of Charles I shows the king with two gauntlets (armoured gloves). Nothing wrong with that, of course, except that he painted two right-hand gauntlets rather than one of each!

Right, not wrong!

People often use King Canute as an example of a power-crazed fool who mistakenly thought that he could control nature. In fact (according to the legend), he was quite the opposite. Canute put up his hand and ordered the waves to stop to show his courtiers that he was just a person and that there was no way that the waves would do as they were told. And he was right.* He got very wet.

> A good point well made, your Majesty.

* And we're wrong to think that he was wrong when he wasn't!

24

The dangers of bathing

Marat was one of the leaders of the French Revolution. His arch-enemies had been the Girondists* but, by the end of May 1793, he had defeated them. And so began the Reign of Terror, in which not only the nobility but also his revolutionary rivals were rooted out and executed. Marat's obsession with trying to weed out the very last of these Girondists led to a fatal error of judgement on his part.

Marie-Anne Charlotte Corday D'Armont was one of a rare breed: a noblewoman by birth who openly supported the revolution. The revolution? Yes. Marat? No. She was a Girondist. Charlotte Corday (as she preferred to be called) was horrified by the terror and took it upon herself to assassinate Marat.

She called at Marat's house on three occasions. Twice she was turned away. The third time she called she pretended to have a list of Girondists who were hiding in Normandy, and insisted she would

* Revolutionaries with many members from the Bordeaux region of the Gironde

only give the names to Marat in person.

Marat was so eager to get his hands on those names that he received Charlotte Corday while he was still in his (tin) bath. She hadn't even been searched. While he was busy writing down the names she gave him she stabbed him in the heart. It was 13 July 1793. She herself was executed just four days later.

Tell it how it isn't . . .

It was probably a mistake for the Scandinavian vacuum-cleaner manufacturer Electrolux to use the slogan 'Nothing sucks like an Electrolux' in its US advertising campaign. In America, 'it sucks' means that it's rubbish!

The baby-food manufacturer Gerber made a mistake with pictures rather than words. They used the same packaging in Africa as in the US for one of their products, showing a baby on the label. As many people in poor regions of Africa are unable to read, most manufacturers put a picture on the label of what's inside the tin . . .

When the Pope visited Spain, an American company decided to cash in on the event by printing special T-shirts for sale there . . . except that instead of reading: 'I saw the Pope' (*el Papa*) they read: 'I saw the Potato' (*la Papa*)!

In a jam

There's no denying that motor racing is a dangerous sport, but just getting to the Targa Florio race meeting in Sicily in 1919 proved hazardous for some. Contestant Enzo Ferrari got his car stuck in snow in the mountains and, if that weren't bad enough, he was surrounded by slavering wolves. Fortunately he had a revolver with him so he managed to keep them off him! If he hadn't, we might never have had Ferrari cars.

On the 'ead, son!

The future Louis XIII – yup, that's unlucky 13 – was dropped on his head when he was a baby. Back then, it was all the rage to carry royal babies around on fancy cushions, and his father made the fumble when he was handed the cushion to give the tiny prince a kiss. Unfortunately His Majesty was left holding not the baby but a lonesome cushion while baby Louis took a nosedive to the floor. After that, a velvet pocket was sewn into the cushion so that the baby prince could be carried around in it like a baby kangaroo in its mother's pouch.*

* An animal unknown to the French court at the time, of course

What's up with those Watsons (and beyond)?

Nowhere in the stories written by his creator, Sir Arthur Conan Doyle, does Sherlock Holmes say, 'Elementary, my dear Watson!' though this is a line used again and again to sum up the flavour of the stories. Mr Holmes didn't say, 'Come here, Watson, I want you!' either. Those were, according to Alexander Graham Bell, the words he said in the world's first phone call. Bell called them out when he spilled acid from a battery on his trousers when experimenting with his telephonic equipment! His assistant Thomas Watson (not a doctor) heard them through his receiver in the other room.

Another Thomas Watson – then chairman of the computer giant IBM – is often quoted as having said, 'I think there is a world market for maybe five computers.' There were around one BILLION (1,000,000,000) PCs by the end of 2008. But let's not be too hard on Mr Watson. IBM claims that his comment was taken out of context so didn't mean that at all. As late as 1977, the founder, president and chairman of Digital Equipment Corp, Ken Olson, said, 'There is no reason anyone would want a computer in their home.' Bill Gates, however, claims that he never made the blunder of saying: '640 kB ought to be enough [computer memory] for anyone.' 'I've said some stupid things and some wrong things,' he commented. 'But not that.'

 As for the Western Union telegraph company though, when it was offered a telephone company for $100,000 its president really did turn it down, saying, 'What use could this company make of an electrical toy?' A Western Union company memo of 1876 read: 'This "telephone" has too many shortcomings to be seriously considered as a means of communication. The device is inherently of no value to us.'

Things we know we don't know . . .

Donald Rumsfeld was the US Secretary of Defense. In 2003 he said, 'Reports that say that something hasn't happened are always interesting to me, because as we know, there are known knowns; there are things we know we know. We also know there are known unknowns; that is to say we know there are some things we do not know. But there are also unknown unknowns – the ones we don't know we don't know.'

This was seen as a load of utter nonsense and/or pants, a real howler. Rumsfeld even went on to be given an Award for Gobbledegook from the Plain English Campaign . . . which I reckon was a mistake. If you think about it, it actually makes perfect sense:

(1) There are things we know we know.*

(2) There are things we know we don't know.**

* For example, most of the universe is made up of 'dark matter'
** For example, exactly what dark matter is

(3) There are things we have no idea we know nothing about.*

* For example, our universe may be in the middle of a giant's cheese sandwich, but we live in blissful ignorance

Nudes news

Wilhelm Roentgen discovered X-rays in 1895 and, almost at once, people misunderstood what they could do. There were fears that 'peeping Toms' would wear X-ray specs so that they could look through people's clothes and stare at their naughty-naked-nude bodies!

As a result, a law was introduced in New Jersey, USA, banning the use of 'X-ray opera glasses', and in London you could buy what was sold as being 'X-ray-proof underwear'! In fact, X-rays go right through skin and can be used to photograph bones.

The hero of Daniel Defoe's *Robinson Crusoe* was a castaway on a desert island. Famously, at one stage, he decided to swim out to the ship-wreck to try to salvage some goods that might be useful to him. Defoe, as Crusoe, wrote:

'I resolved, if possible, to get to the ship; so I pulled off my clothes, for the weather was hot to extremity and took to the water.' Once Robinson Crusoe was aboard the ship: 'I found that all the ship's provisions were dry; and being well disposed to eat, I went to the bread

room and filled my pockets with biscuits.'

Pockets, hmmm? Isn't he in the naughty-naked-nude?! This is often given as an example of a mistake made by the author.

So did Daniel Defoe make a terrible blunder? Not according to a certain Howard R. Garis who wrote to *The New York Times* in 1902 to point out that nowhere does Defoe say that Crusoe took off ALL his clothes. And, anyway, just a few paragraphs AFTER stripping, Crusoe sees his clothes floating by. 'As for my breeches [. . .] I swam on board in them and my stockings.' So *that's* where the pockets came from.

Salad?

Julius Caesar was never Emperor of Rome*
and the Caesar salad wasn't named after him.
The salad was named after its apparent creator,
Caesar Cardini (1896–1956), an Italian who
emigrated to the US but who had a restaurant
in Mexico (probably so that he could still
serve alcohol during prohibition** in the US).
It's claimed that he came up with the dish in
Mexico in 1924 (possibly on 4 July). Some
who worked closely with Cardini claim the
original recipe as their own.

* Caesar Augustus was Rome's first emperor and, as
Julius's nephew, came to power after Julius Caesar's
death
** When drinking alcohol was banned

Into the valley of Death . . . and out the other side

Alfred, Lord Tennyson's famous poem 'The Charge of The Light Brigade' includes the line, 'Into the valley of Death rode the six hundred' (though the actual figure was somewhere between 661 and 673). Most people mistakenly assume that few if any of these men survived.

In fact, only 118 men actually died, less than 18 per cent. In her novel *Black Beauty*, Anna Sewell describes the charge from the point of view of one of the horses.*

* Around 335 horses died as a result of the charge

Pieces of eight! Pieces of eight!

It's been claimed that the US dollar sign $ was based on the letters US (for United States). It's far more likely that it was a variation on the number 8 stamped on pieces of eight* before the North American currency was adopted.

* Yup, those coins Long John Silver's parrot, Captain Flint, was always squawking on about in *Treasure Island*

We have no bananas!

After the end of the First World War, the Versailles Peace Conference was held in 1919. Apparently, British Prime Minister (Welshman) Lloyd George came up with a great way for Italy to rebuild its shattered economy: to grow more bananas. The only problem with this otherwise excellent idea was that the Italians didn't grow bananas in the first place.

A right pickle!

In the US, oil was first discovered in 1829. Dr John Croghan was looking for salt brine (to pickle meat with) and found oil instead. He was very disappointed. What use was oil? The best he could do was bottle it and sell the bottles for 40 cents each, claiming that the oil cured just about anything and everything. It wasn't a great moneymaker!

By now, people were beginning to use paraffin-oil lamps, which gave off much more light than candles. In 1859, Edwin L. Drake realized that there was, therefore, a growing market for oil. In the US, people got oil from deposits seeping out of the ground. Drake decided to drill for it. He persuaded some businessmen to join him in funding the drilling of the world's first oil well. It was sunk – digging slowly, slowly down – in Titusville, Pennsylvania. People came to laugh at 'Drake's Folly'. Some even brought a picnic and made a day of it.

When the drill was 20 metres down, the pump began to suck out oil. Edwin L. Drake was the first person in history to strike oil this way. He should have had the last laugh but, sadly, didn't. His oil company was soon bought by one of his rivals. Drake quit the oil business and, later in life, had to rely on his state pension. By 1890, John D. Rockefeller's Standard Oil Company controlled 90 per cent of the USA's oil! Unlike Dr John Croghan, he'd found a great way to make money from what came to be called 'black gold'.

Shh! Want to know a secret?

During the Second World War, one of the most feared groups of people was Germany's Nazi special police force, the Schutzstaffel – more commonly known as the SS. Less than four years after the war had ended, an English children's book was published centred around a group of children holding secret meetings in a shed with 'SS' labelled proudly on the door.

A howler? A blunder? A terrible mistake?

Obviously not. The mistake was to think that. The book was written by Enid Blyton and 'SS' stood for Secret Seven.* It turned into the first of a series of 15 books that sold in millions around the world.**

* Peter, Jack, Barbara, George, Pam, Colin and Janet**
** The last book, *Fun for the Secret Seven*, was published in 1963. (Enid Blyton died in 1967)***
*** And honorary eighth member Scamper (the dog)****
**** In Blyton's best-known series, The Famous Five, Timmy the dog actually counted as one of the five

NOTE: In March 1997, *Enid Blyton's Mystery and Suspense Magazine* was launched. Some of the Secret Seven stories were retold in strip-cartoon form (with additional puzzles to solve on every spread). These adventures were adapted  and written by – er – me. I also wrote the 'Detection Section'. In the first issue, some of the 'clues' were missing as the top of the illustration was cropped off the top of the page. Sad to say, the magazine didn't last long!

Bad advice

Henry Ford made the world's first mass-produced automobile* (built on a production line), which meant that many ordinary people could afford to buy one.

In 1903, Horace Rackham, Ford's lawyer, was advised by a president of the Michigan Savings Bank not to invest in his client's company. 'The horse is here to stay,' he declared, 'but the auto is only a novelty – a fad.'

Fortunately for Rackham, he didn't take this advice and bought $5,000-worth of stock in the Ford Motor Company. When he sold it, it was worth $12.5 million!!!**

* That's a car, to you and me
** And that was when $12.5 million was REALLY worth something!

Stop lion to me

The four bronze lions at the base of Nelson's Column in Trafalgar Square sit in a way that no real lion could ever sit. Their legs are positioned in the way dogs sit, not cats (which is what lions are, if big ones).

NOTE: On the subject of Nelson – well, he is at the top of that column* – a lot of people mistakenly think that he wore an eyepatch. There's no evidence that he ever did.

* Nelson's Column was originally thought to be 56 metres high from street level to the tippy-top of his hat. In 2006, it was found to measure just 51 metres

On the toss of a coin

A major Russian spy ring was uncovered in the US in 1953 when someone accidentally gave a paper boy a fake coin in New York. The boy dropped the coin – a nickel – and it fell in half. It was hollow and had a tiny piece of microfilm inside. The boy told his girlfriend and she told her father, who was a police detective . . . and he told the FBI.* Now a major spy hunt was under way.

Eventually the coin was traced to a Russian spy named Reino Häyhänen, but the trail didn't end there. The FBI persuaded Häyhänen to tell them everything he knew or face a very long prison sentence indeed. On the information he gave them, they managed to break up a number of small 'cells' (groups of spies). All that was left was to try to track down the spymaster, code-name 'Mark'.

The mysterious 'Mark' had made a mistake of his own. He had once taken Häyhänen to a room where he kept his photographic equipment. Häyhänen didn't remember the

* Federal Bureau of Investigation

address but gave as many details as he could. Acting on this very patchy information, the FBI eventually homed in on 252 Fulton Street and on a certain Mr Emil Goldfus, whom Häyhänen then identified as being 'Mark' from a photograph.

Among the spy gadgets the FBI found in the Fulton Street building were a number of hollow containers made to look like pens, pencils, screws, nails, cufflinks and, of course, coins.

Emil Goldfus wasn't what he seemed to be either. He was, in fact, Rudolf Ivanovitch Abel, a colonel in the KGB.* And he'd been caught because a paper boy had been given the wrong coin.

* Russia's international espionage organization

Name in the frame

In October 2008, Aarron Evans, 21, was sentenced to seven months in prison for breaking into a car in a multi-storey car park in Bristol and stealing satnav equipment. What Evans didn't know was that the car was a 'covert capture car', which had been placed there by the police as bait to catch thieves. Evans was caught on camera and pleaded guilty. What made the police's task that much easier was the tattoo on his neck, clearly seen on the video. It read: 'EVANS 19-9-87' – the thief's name and date of birth!

A not-so-helpful helping hand

One of the most extraordinary Olympic marathons was the one held during the 1908 London games. The first to cross the finishing line – in what later became known as the 'Dorando marathon' – was Italian pastry-cook Dorando Pietri. Pietri, a small man, was an amazing runner. At 17, he once delivered an urgent message for his employer by running the 15 miles! This was the start of an impressive running career. He ran, and won, a number of marathons and then came the 1908 London Olympics.

The day of the race was a hot one. The course of just over 26 miles ran from Windsor Castle to the White City Stadium. The streets were lined with a quarter of a million spectators.

Dorando Pietri was up with the leaders from the outset and, with the finishing line in sight, streaked into the lead, with American runner John Hayes close behind. As he entered the stadium, Pietri was suffering from heat exhaustion. He kept falling and struggling back to his feet and falling down again . . .

. . . It was now that Olympic officials (obviously impressed by Pietri's get-up-and-go) rushed across the track, picked him up and helped him across the finishing line.

When John Hayes crossed the line moments later, it was he who was declared the winner. The officials' help had disqualified Pietri.

The crowd was horrified. The Olympic officials – who should have known better – had made a serious blunder, having been caught up in the excitement and drama of the moment.

But rules are rules.

Pietri may not have won the gold medal (or silver or bronze, come to that) but he was eventually presented with a special cup by Queen Alexandra.

Biting the bullet

There's a trick where a magician appears to catch a bullet fired from a gun between his teeth, but there's one thing you can be sure of: that's not what really happens.

Another variation of the trick is when the conjurer holds up a plate in front of his chest. Two bullets are then fired by a two-man firing squad, which the magician miraculously catches in the plate without it breaking . . . though that wasn't the case for Chung Ling Soo at the Wood Green Empire on 23 March 1918. Instead, one of the bullets smashed through the china and killed him.

The key secret of the trick was in the rifles. When the real bullets had been pushed down the barrels, they fell into a small chamber safely out of the way, and harmless blanks were fired in their place . . . However, over time, one of these chambers had filled up with old gunpowder – from the trick being repeated again and again over the years – and the real bullet remained in the barrel and was actually fired at Chung Ling Soo.*

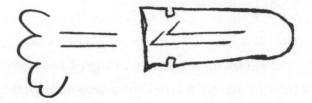

* Chung Ling Soo's other secret was that, despite his name, he wasn't really Chinese. He wore traditional Chinese robes on stage and was made up to look Chinese, but his real name was William Ellsworth Robinson and he was American with Scottish ancestry

A botched job?
Divine intervention?
Extraordinary luck?

The year was 1803 and the country was Australia. Repeat offender Joseph Samuels had been found guilty of murder and was due to be executed. The method of execution was hanging: he stood on a cart underneath the gallows with a rope around his neck. When the time came, a pair of horses would pull the cart out from under him.

A crowd had gathered to watch and in that crowd Samuels saw a familiar face. It belonged to Isaac Simmonds, the man he was sure had actually committed the murder of which he'd been found guilty! From the cart beneath the gallows, Samuels declared his own innocence and accused Simmonds of being the killer.

Amazingly, the crowd was suddenly on Samuels's side. People became restless, demanding Samuels's release. The person in charge of the hanging, the Provost Marshal, had to act quickly. He ordered that the horses pull the cart out from under Samuels.

With the cart gone, Samuels dropped and
the rope tightened around his neck . . . only
to break moments later.* He fell to the
ground unharmed. Now the crowd swarmed
forward and had to be kept back by soldiers
with bayonets fixed to the end of their
rifles.

Quickly a new rope was found and Samuels
found himself back on the cart with his head
through a second noose. For a second time,
the horses were whipped and dashed forward,
pulling the cart out from under him.

This time the rope didn't break. Something
even more incredible happened. The new rope
began to unwind into its separate strands,
causing Joseph Samuels to spin slowly to the
ground.

The crowd was dumbfounded. After a moment
of stunned silence, people began baying for
Samuels's release. Again the Provost Marshal
ignored them and for a THIRD time they

* The rope, that is – not his neck

attempted to hang Samuels . . . and AGAIN the rope snapped.

This time, the Provost Marshal ordered Samuels be taken back to his cell while he reported the amazing turn of events to the Governor. He also had the ropes tested.* They seemed fine. The third rope had weights of 190 kilogrammes (just under 30 stone) hung from it without breaking.

The governor granted Joseph Samuels a reprieve. Samuels was the first person to be hanged three times and live to tell the tale. The murder case was reopened and the authorities admitted they'd made a mistake. None other than Isaac Simmonds – the face in the crowd – was later brought to trial.

* Well, you would, wouldn't you? I'll bet by now you were suspecting that the ropes were dodgy

Dogged by bad luck

As well as being a great conductor of classical music, Otto Klemperer was also extraordinarily accident-prone and a victim of bad health. Once, when rehearsing in a Leipzig concert hall, he leaned on the railing of the conductor's podium, which broke. He fell to the ground, knocking himself unconscious.

After moving to America, in 1939, an operation to remove a tumour left him partially paralysed and with a 'twisted' face, leading to rumours that he had suffered a nervous breakdown and escaped from a lunatic asylum!

In 1951, Klemperer was about to climb on board a plane for Europe when he slipped on the tarmac and broke his hip. As a result, he spent eight months in hospital and it was FOUR years before he could again conduct standing up!

It was in Zurich, Switzerland, in 1959 that he had his most extraordinary accident. The conductor fell asleep while smoking a cigarette, setting the bedclothes on fire. When he woke up, he snatched the water jug from his bedside table and poured the contents on the flames . . .

. . . only it wasn't his water jug but spirits of camphor – highly inflammable oil – or, some say, whisky! He was very seriously burned and for a while it was thought that he might not survive. But he did . . . in time to fall (again) and break his hip (again)!

Having SO many accidents would be strange enough, but the involvement of a black dog (or dogs) adds a whole new level of weirdness.

There was the black dog which entered the Leipzig concert hall moments before he fell from the podium; the black dog that bounded across the tarmac of the runway, causing him to slip and break his hip; the black dog he claimed to have been dreaming about ☞

when his bedclothes caught light; the black dog he saw before he broke a hip a second time . . .

. . . like the black dog that jumped up on to his shoulders in 1888 when he was a small boy out walking with his parents,* knocking him to the ground.

As Otto Klemperer himself later said: 'Since then I have always been frightened of dogs. Again and again, in various forms, I have seen this black dog, or ones very much like it, shortly before disaster has struck at me . . .'

One dog or many? Clumsiness, bad luck or fate?

* This was in his home town, Breslau, which was in Germany. It was later renamed Wroclaw when it became a part of Poland**
** As he was Jewish, he fled to Switzerland before the Second World War

Snow on their boots

In August 1914, a train packed with soldiers pulled into a country station in southern England. According to one version of events, a porter asked one of the men where they'd come from, and the Scottish soldier replied, 'Ross-shire.' The porter thought he'd said Russia – an ally of Britain in the First World War – and so a rumour began. Soon it grew with the telling, with people reporting that the soldiers were definitely Russians because they'd seen snow on their boots.*

This mistake actually fooled a German spy! Carl Lody (in England using a passport stolen from American Charles Inglis) heard the rumour of Russian troop movements and went to check them out. He too witnessed soldiers passing through and mistakenly assumed that they were, indeed, Russians.** He sent

* Quite why this snow hadn't melted somewhere between Russia and England was a question left unasked
** British marines wore blue uniforms and peakless caps at the time, not that different from Russian uniforms

a written report to another spy, in Sweden. British Intelligence had been watching him for a while and intercepting his mail. However, because this report contained false information – suggesting that Britain might actually have more troops on hand than it did – it was allowed through unaltered.

Arrested in October 1914, Lody didn't deny his actions. He was a German working for Germany and was proud of it. He was shot at dawn on 6 November in the Tower of London.

Tears of a clown

John Abernethy was a well-respected British doctor and teacher. Famously, on one occasion, a patient came to see him, claiming to feel depressed. Dr Abernethy thought he had the perfect remedy. He suggested that the man go and watch the clown Grimaldi, who'd be far better medicine than anything out of a bottle.

'I am Grimaldi,' replied the man.*

* I really, REALLY hope this story is true. I first heard a version of it as a boy and have been itching to include it in a book for YEARS. John Abernethy certainly lived from 1764 to 1831, and (Joseph) Grimaldi from 1778 to 1837, but who knows whether this conversation ever took place

Head over heels

The painter Wassily Kandinsky is said to have completely changed his style of painting because of a mistake. Once, when walking through a gallery (or possibly his own studio), he stopped to admire an unfamiliar painting. He stared at it for quite a while, appreciating its 'extraordinary beauty glowing with an inner radiance' . . .

. . . until it suddenly dawned on him that he was looking at one of his own works hanging the wrong way up!* The 'look' that he saw in the upside-down picture inspired him to try painting abstracts.

* Some people swear that in 1961 MoMA, the Museum of Modern Art in New York, hung the painting *Le Bateau* (*The Boat*) by Henri Matisse the wrong way up for forty-seven days. (You can see how this might have happened, what with the subject being a boat with its mirror image reflected in the water below.) Others claims it's lies, all lies!

The right way up?

Upside down?

63

A copper-bottomed discovery

Iodine, an element which is now used in everything from medicines to water purifiers to food preservatives to wool dye to the coating on sunglasses to heaven knows what else, was discovered completely by mistake.

In 1811, Napoleon Bonaparte was planning to invade Russia and needed more gunpowder. An important ingredient in making gunpowder is saltpetre, and he was finding it hard to lay his hands on large enough quantities.

A French chemist, Courtois, got it into his head that seaweed could contain saltpetre and he needed to find a way of extracting it. He boiled large quantities of seaweed in a copper pot to collect the liquid it gave off. What was far more interesting, however, was what he found when he emptied the pot: its lining was badly corroded.

After more experimentation, Courtois was left with a black powder, which he was hoping might be some all-new explosive to please the emperor. When he heated it, however, the black powder turned to violet vapour then to black crystalline flakes . . . He had discovered iodine.*

It wasn't until 1830 that a French doctor discovered that liquid extracted from iodine flakes helped protect wounds from infection. Since then, it's probably done a lot more good for the world than gunpowder ever could.

* So-called because it comes from the Greek *iodes*, meaning violet

That sinking feeling

Rose Greenhow was a well-respected member of fashionable American society. During the American Civil War, however, she was also a Confederate spy. People thought that she was a loyal Unionist (wanting to keep America's states united), when she was really fighting for the cause of the breakaway southern states.

Greenhow made an excellent spy until she caught the attention of Allan Pinkerton,* whom President Abraham Lincoln had put in charge of the Unionists' counter-intelligence service. He kept an eye on her and eventually had her placed under house arrest.**

This didn't stop her getting messages to her Confederate colleagues though. She hid them in gifts to 'friends' and even wove tapestries containing secret (colour-coded) information.

Rose Greenhow's reputation spread and she

* Founder of the world-famous Pinkerton Detective Agency, he died of an infection in 1884 after biting his tongue
** As the name suggests, this meant that she couldn't leave her home

soon earned the nickname 'Rebel Rose'. In 1862, she was moved to a proper prison . . . but was eventually released.

Once free, she managed to get past the Union warships trying to block Confederate ships from coming and going and sailed to England as an ambassador for the breakaway cause. There she wrote a book about her spying and even got to meet Queen Victoria.

Then came her big mistake. Rebel Rose had been given plenty of gold coins by people in England sympathetic to the Confederacy. Now that it was time to return to America, she decided to have them sewn into the lining of her dress for safe keeping.

Unfortunately, just off the North Carolina coast of America, her ship was spotted and chased by a Union gunboat. Greenhow jumped into a rowing boat and tried to get ashore, but the boat capsized, tossing her into the rough seas . . .

. . . where she sank like a stone. The gold coins weighed her down. They were her death warrant.

You what?

In the all-time classic film *The Wizard of Oz*, starring Judy Garland as Dorothy, the Cowardly Lion sings the song 'If I Were King', in which he asks, 'What makes the Sphinx the Seventh Wonder?' A strange question when you consider that the Sphinx isn't one of the Seven Wonders of the World!*

The other six wonders are:

The Hanging Gardens of Babylon

The Temple of Artemis at Ephesus

The Statue of Zeus at Olympia

The Mausoleum at Halicarnassus

The Colossus of Rhodes

The Pharos (Lighthouse) of Alexandria

The Great Pyramid is the only one of the Seven Wonders surviving to this day.

* The nearby Great Pyramid at Giza is

Making laws and breaking laws

Today, most countries with a shoreline claim territorial waters three miles out to sea. Within this three-mile limit, foreign vessels are not allowed to enter without permission and, once entered, are not allowed to 'show aggression'. The distance of three miles was the typical range of a 17th-century cannonball.

The idea of territorial waters came from Hugo Grotius, a Dutch scholar, in 1609.* He was not so much interested in protecting a country's territories as stopping countries from claiming too much sea for themselves. He argued that 'no prince [should] challenge farther into the sea than he can command with a cannon', which would allow a much easier passage of ships.

Unluckily for Grotius, he didn't just write about shipping. He also wrote that the Bible shouldn't be taken as complete truth but that parts of it could be understood

* In his legal work *The Free Sea*

to mean a variety of different things. This landed him in Holland's Loevestein Jail* in 1619.

Grotius's wife, Maria, and family were allowed to live there with him, and the authorities let her come and go as she pleased. Hugo Grotius was still respected as a scholar – so long as he steered clear of religion – so they let Maria bring books to the fortress once a month, and return them a month later.

This is where the Dutch authorities made a big boo-boo. The books were always carried in and out in a large trunk.

Yes, t-r-u-n-k, as in BIG ENOUGH TO HIDE GROTIUS INSIDE, which is exactly what Maria persuaded her (somewhat reluctant) husband to do on 22 March 1621**. Two soldiers from the fortress innocently delivered the trunk of 'books' to the house of a friend of Grotius. He then fled to Paris,

* Part of a fortress
** A USEFUL TIP FOR ALL WOULD-BE JAILERS: Always search a trunk when going in or out, just to be sure what – or WHO – is inside!

where his family later joined him.*

Sadly, in 1645, Grotius was a victim of the sea he helped to protect. He was shipwrecked in heavy gales in the Baltic, was washed ashore near Rostock and rescued, but died in a local vicarage.

* It was in Paris that Grotius published *The Law of War and Peace* (which he'd been writing while a prisoner), which recommended ways of settling disputes between countries without their resorting to war. This became the basis for much of today's international law and is probably why the International Court is in Hague in Holland, Hugo Grotius's home country (but I won't swear to it)

A terrible blow

Jim Thorpe, a Native American of the Sauk and Fox tribe, was born in Oklahoma, USA, in 1887. His tribal name was Wa-Tho-Huck. He became the Carlisle Indian School's* best athlete. When Carlisle School met Lafayette School in an athletics competition, Jim Thorpe was Carlisle's ONLY team member. He took part in every event . . . and beat Lafayette's full team!

In the 1912 Stockholm Olympics, Thorpe won gold in both the pentathlon** and the decathlon***, two of the most gruelling events. When receiving his second medal from King Gustav V of Sweden, the king said, 'Sir, you are the world's greatest athlete.'

But today you won't find Jim Thorpe's name in a list of Olympic champions except, perhaps, in a footnote. To take part in the

* In Pennsylvania
** Long jump, javelin, 200 metres, discus, 1,500 metres
*** Long jump, high jump, shot put, javelin, pole vault, discus, 100 metres, 400 metres, 1,500 metres, and the 110-metre hurdles

Olympics, you must be an amateur – have never been paid to take part in sport. Sadly it turned out that, when playing semi-professional baseball some years previously, he'd received a small payment. This disqualified him. (Thorpe hadn't realized this.)

Happily, despite being stripped of his Olympic golds, Jim Thorpe went on to become a top professional baseball player and top American football player and is generally accepted to be one of the greatest athletes of the first half of the 20th century. He died in 1953. There's even a town named after him!

Heads you lose

France's first postage stamp was issued in 1849 and was unpopular with many French people from the start. Firstly, it looked suspiciously like Britain's first postage stamp, the Penny Black, and Britain was traditionally France's rival.* Secondly, there was the choice of the head used on the stamp. The Penny Black showed the head of Queen Victoria but, being a republic, France had no monarch, so the head of Ceres was chosen.

Ceres is the Roman goddess of harvest and prosperity . . . so choosing her seemed more than a little insensitive when France, along with much of Europe, had been going through 'the hungry forties', with poor harvests, poverty and hunger.

No wonder the stamp was soon replaced by one with an entirely new design!

* If not actual enemy

Famous last words

In 1962, an executive from the Decca record label said of the Beatles: 'We don't like their sound, and guitar music is on the way out.'

The Beatles went on to become the most famous band in the history of pop music, with 17 No. 1 singles and 15 No. 1 albums . . . and that's just in the UK charts. Within just TEN years of the executive's howler, the group – John Lennon, Paul McCartney, George Harrison and Ringo Starr* – had sold over 545 million records worldwide!

* Born Richard Starkey

Killing looks

It used to be very fashionable in England for ladies to look as pale as possible. A white face showed that you didn't have to work in the fields; in fact, you didn't have to work at all. Queen Elizabeth I* is famous for plastering her face with white make-up. She used white lead as a foundation, with an enamel made from egg white painted over the top. This wasn't a great idea. It ruined her skin and is probably what caused all her hair to fall out too.

Lead is, of course, highly poisonous and can be absorbed through the skin. In the 18th century, the Countess of Coventry – considered a great beauty in her day – died of lead poisoning from her make-up. She was only 27.

* Queen Elizabeth I was very particular as to how she appeared in portraits, so all painters were provided with a 'mask of beauty': a kind of template-cum-stencil which they had to follow

Don't lose your bottle!

When a junior officer in the 11th Hussars made the simple mistake of placing a bottle of wine on the officers' mess table instead of a decanter, it triggered a series of events that were to end in a trial in the House of Lords for attempted murder!

The year was 1840, and the commander of the 11th Hussars was the famously short-tempered Lord Cardigan.* Cardigan flew into a rage over the bottle being put on the table, so much so that he had Captain Reynolds, the young officer who'd made the mistake, placed under military arrest!

When journalist Captain Harvey Tuckett heard about this overreaction he wrote an article about it in the *Morning Chronicle*,

* James Thomas Brudenell, 7th Earl of Cardigan**
** After whom the knitted waistcoat-type-thingy is named***
***and who fought at the Battle of Balaclava, which gave its name to another knitted garment: a kind of helmet. (These were sent to British soldiers to keep them warm during the Crimean War)

pointing out how ridiculous Cardigan was being . . . and ended up being challenged to a duel by the man himself.

Duelling was no longer seen as the gentlemanly thing to do in England so, when Lord Cardigan shot Mr Tuckett, wounding him, he was tried in the House of Lords in 1841.

The trial didn't even last a whole day. Cardigan was found not guilty by his fellow lords, mainly on a technicality: Harvey Tuckett's full name hadn't been correctly entered on the charge sheet.

This caused mutterings in the press about there being one rule for the rich and one for ordinary folk, and the whole 'black bottle affair' did not show his lordship in a very good light. He and his regiment were, apparently, plagued by people whispering or shouting, 'Black bottle!' when they passed.

Later in life, Lord Cardigan was involved in a number of famous battles* and went out of his way to make clear what a hero he'd been. Others involved saw things differently.

* It was Lord Cardigan who, among other things, led the ill-fated charge of the Light Brigade

The real thing

What do the following fictional characters have in common?

 The lover Casanova

 The big-nosed duellist Cyrano de Bergerac

The teller-of-tall-tales Baron Munchausen

The answer? That, despite what many people think, they're not actually fictional characters! Elements of their lives have been fictionalized, but they were living, breathing people.

Giacomo Girolamo Casanova de Seingalt lived from 1725 to 1798, Hector Savinien de Cyrano de Bergerac from 1619 to 1655 and Karl Friedrich Hieronymous Freiherr von Münchhausen from 1720 to 1797.

Food on your family

Former US president George W. Bush is famous for his howlers.* Here are my top five from the year 2000 alone:

'Rarely is the question asked: Is our children learning?'
South Carolina, 11 January

'I know how hard it is for you to put food on your family.'
New Hampshire, 27 January

'I know the human being and fish can coexist peacefully.'
Michigan, 29 September

'Families is where our nation finds hope, where wings take dream.'
Winsconsin, 18 October

'They misunderestimated me.'
Arkansas, 6 November

* As well as saying strange things, George W. Bush did some strange things too, such as giving the German Chancellor a neck massage – without her asking for one! – at an important summit meeting in 2006

Stuffed

Sir Francis Bacon,* the 17th-century polymath,** was interested in seeing if food could be preserved by freezing it. One day he stuffed a chicken carcass with freshly frozen snow. Unfortunately, he caught a chill and died from it . . . so his experiment remained uncompleted.

* Probably most famous for not really being Shakespeare
** OK, OK. Get the jokes about 'parrots good with figures' out of the way. A polymath is actually someone who's good at lots of things***
*** Rather than a jack of all trades and master of none

Some pig!

The saying 'Never buy a pig in a poke'* means 'Be sure of what you're getting.' This dates back to a time when people would stuff a ('worthless') stray cat in a sack and try to sell it as a pig to an unsuspecting innocent.** According to legend, however, an actual pig helped save the town of Carcassonne in southern France.

The story goes that, in AD 795, the fortress town was under siege from the Emperor Charlemagne's forces. They had surrounded the town and were sitting tight, planning to starve the townsfolk into surrendering.

After five years, all that was left of the food supplies was one scrawny pig and one sack of grain. Soon the town would have to surrender. But the town's leader, Dame Carcas, wasn't about to give up. She had a plan. She took the pig and fed it all the grain

* A poke is a bag or a sack. (I bet you could have worked that out for yourself)
** Which is also where the phrase 'Letting the cat out of the bag' comes from, meaning giving the game away!

(much to the horror of some people, who thought she'd gone crazy). They should be eating the grain and the pig, not feeding one to the other!

When the pig was as plump as could be, Dame Carcas stood on the fortified walls and, asking if they were hungry, threw the pig down to Charlemagne's forces, who couldn't believe their eyes. They made the mistake of believing that, if the people in Carcassonne could afford to fatten up a pig and toss it away, they must have plenty of food in there, and the siege could go on for much, much longer! They packed up their tents and left.

The town was saved.*

* Or so goes the legend, anyway

84

Bungled in the bunker

On 20 July 1944, Colonel Claus von
Stauffenberg, Chief of Staff of Germany's
home army, attempted to assassinate Adolf
Hitler by placing his briefcase – containing
a bomb – under a table in Wolf's Lair,
the Führer's secret underground bunker.
Stauffenberg managed to position the 2 lb
(0.9 kg) bomb – with just a five-minute fuse –
then leave. When he'd left the bunker, another
member of staff accidentally kicked the
briefcase up against a thick iron table support,
which acted as a shield. When the bomb
exploded, Adolf Hitler survived. Stauffenberg
wasn't so lucky. He and nine of his fellow
plotters were arrested and executed. Had their
plan not been bungled, who knows how much
sooner the Second World War might have
ended?

Not a leg to stand on

Australia's most famous outlaw was Ned Kelly, their very own man in the iron mask.* As well as his home-made helmet, he also wore body armour covering his torso, and he acted as though he was indestructible. His fatal blunder, however, was that he didn't think it necessary to protect his LEGS! This was his downfall.**

After a couple of years robbing banks and even raiding whole towns, Ned Kelly and his gang*** were finally surrounded in an inn in Glenrowan, a town in the state of Victoria. After an

* Which was shaped a bit like a small postbox with a slit to look out of, rather than post letters through
** Both literally and metaphorically
*** Imaginatively named the Kelly Gang

eight-hour gun battle with the authorities, Kelly made a break for freedom. Wearing his cumbersome armour, he wasn't agile enough to jump on to a horse so decided to run for it. He was shot in the legs, fell to the ground and was captured.

Once he was well enough to stand trial, Ned Kelly was tried and hanged in Melbourne in 1880. Some saw him as a Robin Hood-type romantic hero, others as a ruthless thief and murderer.* Either way, he's still one of Australia's most famous sons.

* The Kelly Gang's victims included three policemen

A race to the finish

A two-car race intended to take the participants 17,500 miles from Cape North at the extreme tip of Norway to Cape Town in South Africa was fraught with dangers . . . and blunders. Englishman Richard Pape originally set off in July 1955 with Norwegian co-driver Johan Brun. Unfortunately, Brun became seriously ill and had to be taken to an RAF hospital. Pape, meanwhile, had to find a replacement co-driver as soon as possible.

RAF Sergeant Johnny Johnson volunteered and soon the two men were back in the race. Near Tangiers, their car was in serious need of repairs after being driven over so many pot-holes, but they made it to the Bou Denib* . . .

. . . only to be arrested by the French Foreign Legion! Richard Pape was suspected of being a spy, while Johnny Johnson was arrested as a deserter!

Sergeant Johnson was sent back to his base and, once again, Pape was on his own AND

* A fortified Moroccan village

also discovered that there was now a third car in the race.

Pape's worst mistake was probably his most understandable. Following a crash and on foot in the Sahara Desert in the middle of a sandstorm, he became delirious and was taken in by a mirage of an oasis, imagining cool shade and water where there was none. Fortunately, on finding nothing but yet more sand, he had the presence of mind to fire his revolver in the air to attract attention.

He was rescued by some passing camel drivers and, following some more hair-raising and incredible adventures, went on to win the race on 22 October of the same year.

If such a race was considered today, one of the key elements would be the choice of vehicle: probably an all-terrain 4 x 4 tailor-made or adapted for the specific conditions. Richard Pape – already a war hero and bestselling author – made his incredible journey in nothing more than an Austin A90, a bog-standard family car!

Lost for words

In 1877, US president Ulysses S. Grant decided to take a world cruise so that he could address the people of many nations. Unfortunately, not as much meeting and greeting went on as he might have hoped. His false teeth fell overboard and he didn't have a spare pair!

Seeing stars

Grand Central Station in New York is one of the most famous railway terminals in the world and has appeared as a location in numerous films, both live-action and animated.* Under its golden clock has been a popular spot to meet for millions of people over the years.

The ceiling of the main concourse is covered with a depiction of a number of constellations which, for some unexplained reason, have been painted back to front! To try and get around this muddle, when the ceiling was cleaned in the 1990s, a new plaque was added stating:

'Said to be backwards, it's actually seen from a point of view outside our solar system.'**

* Including the amazing dance sequence in *The Fisher King* and the capturing of the escaped zoo animals in *Madagascar*
** Which sounds like a bit of a cop-out to me!

By gum!

When Yorkshireman Jemmy Hirst met King George III he didn't quite follow royal etiquette. Instead, he shook the king vigorously by the hand, declaring, 'Well, I'm right glad to see thee such a plain owd chap,' but His Majesty didn't seem bothered by this howler. The royal personage had heard all about this weird and allegedly wonderful plain-speaking man. In fact, when Hirst had received a letter asking him to go to London to see the king, his rambling reply asked, 'What does His Majesty want to see me for? I'm nothing related to him.' He then went on to say that he was 'busy just now'.

Jemmy Hirst was a bit of a nutter, by all accounts, or liked to behave like one (which is odd in its own way too). He once jumped from the mast of a ship moored in the River Humber. He had a set of home-made wings strapped to his back and his intention, apparently, was to fly. He didn't succeed.

He also used to travel around the highways and byways of the Yorkshire countryside in

a boat on wheels while wearing a special hat
with an ENORMOUS brim.

One of his most famous possessions though
was a glass coffin with automatic closing
doors and a bell. People couldn't resist asking
to try it out, and Hirst was always happy to
oblige. Once inside, he'd only release them for
an exit fee.

He finally needed a coffin himself in 1829,
when he died at the ripe old age of 91. At his
funeral he wanted to be carried by twelve 'old
maids' to the tune of *O'er the Hills and Far
Away*. Only two willing maids could be found.

Look out belowwwwwww!

In 13th-century China, men were sometimes strapped to huge kites so that they could be flown above enemy lines during battles to report back on troop movements. A great idea – so long as the wind didn't drop.

Splat.

A catastrophe

For some extraordinary reason almost beyond comprehension, in 1879, the authorities in Liège, Belgium, got it into their heads that cats might be good at delivering the post.

I'll pause so you can read that paragraph again.

Yes: cats delivering the mail.

They attempted to train 37 cats to deliver letters within a 19-mile radius of the town. They were fitted out with little bags containing the letters and let loose on the population. Of course, the result was inevitable. The cats did what cats do best: whatever they felt like! The idea was soon abandoned.

Not so well red

When tomatoes were first grown in England they were for decoration only. People thought these 'love apples' looked pretty, but they wouldn't dream of eating one. Tomatoes were assumed to be poisonous!

By the horn

Powdered unicorn horn has always been extremely expensive for two reasons: its imagined magical properties (especially useful for medicines) and its incredible rarity. Perhaps the main reason it's so difficult to get your hands on any is because there's no such thing as a unicorn.

When traveller Marco Polo first laid eyes on a rhinoceros, he thought this was a unicorn and was very disappointed how ugly a 'real' one was compared to the unicorns in art and stories. What many people mistook for a unicorn horn was the horn from a narwhal*, sometimes washed ashore.

* A small Arctic whale, the male of which has a forward-pointing corkscrew tusk

Cherry, ma chérie?

Napoleon Bonaparte* may be France's most famous general and emperor but – er – he wasn't actually French. He was from the island of Corsica, off what is now Italy. As well as being famous for being small, sticking one arm in his jacket and saying, 'Not tonight, Josephine,' to his first wife, as a young man Napoleon wasn't too good at expressing affection.

In 1785, aged 16,** he met a girl by the name of Caroline de Colombier and wanted them to be girlfriend and boyfriend.*** The only way he could express his interest was by eating cherries with her. Surprise, surprise, the relationship didn't go anywhere.

Some people believe that Napoleon was murdered by the British. The weapon?

* His surname started out as Buonaparte with a 'u', but he changed it to make it look and sound French
** By which time he'd earned the nickname 'straw-nose Napoleon'
*** He was obviously very fond of her, writing to her regularly later in life, even after she'd married someone else!

Poisonous wallpaper. It could have been an accident, of course. The colour green in wallpaper at the time was often made using the poison arsenic!!!

Snappy dresser

Explorer Mary Kingsley (1862–1900) was
the sister of Charles Kingsley, who wrote
a famous book called *The Water Babies*.
She was an explorer (who enjoyed a bit of
mountain-climbing and canoeing along the
way). Her best-known adventures were in west
Africa, where she claimed to have been given
the nickname 'Only me' by black Africans: the
words she used when entering their villages.

Miss Kingsley once made the mistake of
annoying an angry crocodile, but was saved

by her strict Victorian dress code. She insisted on wearing normal ladies' clothing* during her explorations and – according to her own accounts – was saved from the croc's teeth by the thickness of her 'voluminous skirts'!

* Being in the middle of a jungle, swamp or desert would be no excuse for a true lady to be wearing shorts or trousers!

An official cover-up

When Michelangelo* painted *The Last Judgement* in the Sistine Chapel in Rome he whipped up quite a storm by painting everyone naked.** Pope Paul III wasn't at all happy about it and neither were his successors. Michelangelo was told to add clothes on a number of occasions but chose to ignore these demands, until he received an official written papal order. At first he still resisted making any changes . . . but going against a pope was a dangerous game to play. In the end he instructed one of his promising assistants (Daniele da Volterra) to add clothes to some – but by no means all – of the naked bodies.

Da Volterra started his task in 1565 and the papal authorities were satisfied (although he didn't get to finish because his equipment was removed from the chapel for Pope Pius IV's funeral in 1566). The trouble was that by then

* Full name Michelangelo di Lodovico Buonarroti Simoni
** He started work some time between 1534 and 1537 and completed it in 1541

fashions had changed. Nude bodies were 'in', Michelangelo was seen as a genius, and da Volterra was thereafter known as Il Braghettone ('the Breeches Maker')*: the man who'd painted clothes over parts of a masterpiece!

* 'Breeches' is Olde-Worlde-speak for 'trousers'

'I'll be back!'

As a young man, Julius Caesar was captured by pirates in the Aegean Sea while on his way to Rhodes.* The pirates weren't interested in Caesar; they were simply planning to hold him hostage to get MONEY. According to one version of events, when he heard that they were demanding a ransom of 20 talents he got very angry and insisted that they ask for 50!

The pirates treated him well and he was polite back. They even played sports together. But Julius Caesar did warn them that, once the ransom was paid and he'd been released, he would track them down and have them tried and executed.

Their fatal blunder was not taking him seriously.

The ransom was indeed paid. Caesar was indeed released. And he did indeed gather together a group of men who went back with

* 'All Rhodes lead to Rome'**
** A terrible pun***
*** Oh, never mind

him and captured the pirates while they were still busy counting the money! They were tried, found guilty and sentenced to crucifixion.

Because the pirates had treated him reasonably during his kidnapping, Caesar thought crucifixion was rather too slow and painful a death for them, so he had them strangled before they were nailed to their crosses.

Nice guy.

Small print

The tiny Pyrenean state of Andorra was
officially at war with Germany long after the
First World War was over for everyone else.
Britain had already declared war on Germany
in the Second World War by the time Andorra
and Germany finally signed a peace treaty
on 25 September 1939. And why was this?
Because Andorra's name had somehow been
left out of the documents for the Treaty of
Versailles when everyone else made peace!

An ill wind

Once when the Earl of Oxford bowed low as
he was about to leave the presence of Her
Gracious Majesty Queen Elizabeth I, he broke
wind. He was so embarrassed that he left court
– some say the country – for SEVEN years.

When he finally returned to court all
those years later, the queen took
one look at him and said, "My
lord, I had forgot the fart!"

PARP!

107

Gone to his head

In 1907, in a flat above a Bloomsbury baker's shop, eight-year-old John Barbirolli was practising his violin. Badly. So badly in fact that the boy's grandfather snatched the instrument from under John's chin and broke it over the boy's head. Perhaps he was hoping for some peace and quiet.

It didn't work. Yes, Barbirolli gave up the violin, but he took up the cello, an instrument far too large for his grandfather to lift and hit him over the head with . . . and for a long time Barbirolli only knew one tune,* which he played again and again and again.**

Barbirolli's love of music grew and he later switched from being a player to being a conductor, leading the likes of the London Symphony Orchestra and the New York Philharmonic Orchestra and becoming the permanent conductor of the Hallé Orchestra in Manchester. He also became the first conductor to have a regular spot on TV.

* *The Blue Bells of Scotland*
** Which served Grandpa right!

Never surrender

On 1 August 1943, during the Second World War, the Germans shot down a civilian aircraft leaving a neutral country. For many years it was thought that this was because the Germans mistakenly believed that the British prime minister, Winston Churchill, was on board. One of the passengers was, indeed, a large cigar-smoking man with more than a passing ressemblance to Churchill. His name was Alfred Chenhalls and he was the business manager of the world-famous British film star Leslie Howard,* who was with him on the flight. It now seems that Howard was the target of the attack. The star had done a great deal to try to win people from neutral countries over to the Allied cause. He was also, in fact, a British spy, doing far more for Britain than met the eye. He and Chenhalls, along with most people on the plane, were killed.

Interestingly, information on the shooting is classified until 2025.

* Whose films included *Gone with the Wind*

Over a barrel

One of the most famous paintings by Raphael* is the Madonna of the Chair, showing the Madonna** holding the baby Jesus with a young John the Baptist looking on. Part of its beauty is its shape. The picture is circular.

The story goes that Raphael painted it on the lid of a barrel. He'd arrived at an inn, seen a mother and her children and decided to paint them there and then . . . even though he didn't have a canvas. When she had to leave, he thanked the woman and paid her for having modelled for him, then carried on painting.

A little later, he asked the landlord for a meal, which was provided. When it came to paying for it, however, he realized his mistake: he'd given the last of his money to the model! He ended up paying for his meal with the painting itself.*** Today it is worth millions of pounds.

* Real name Raffaelo Sanzio
** The Virgin Mary
*** If this is true, Raphael must've been an incredibly fast painter, or taken the painting away with him to finish before sending it back to the landlord. The whole thing sounds highly unlikely to me. Makes a good story though

A wild horse chase

Back in 1850s America, it was a slow business getting letters between Missouri and California, where the population had grown from practically nothing following the discovery of gold. Not only did the mail have to travel huge distances, but many of these miles were through desert-like plains, over mountains, across rivers and often in 'Indian Country', populated by Native Americans who didn't like the European settlers who'd claimed their land. The fastest mail took 22 days to deliver by stagecoach . . . but all this was about to change.

In 1860 three men – William H. Russell, Alexander Majors and William B. Waddell – started the Pony Express. They built 190 stations, where the riders could change their horses for fresh ones and collect any additional mail. They then bought 500 fast horses and placed advertisements which read:

∽ **WANTED** ∽

young, skinny, wiry fellows, not over 18.
Must be expert riders, willing to risk death daily.
Orphans preferred. Wages $25 a week.

Eighty riders were hired. They had to follow strict rules. There was a ban on swearing and they each had to carry a Bible. They were also given a revolver and a rifle with orders to use them in self-defence only.* They would ride set distances, after which they would hand the mail over to the next rider and so on, until a delivery was complete. For each mail run 75 ponies were used in each direction – there and back.

The idea really caught people's imaginations and the first Pony Express riders were welcomed like heroes. Delivery times were reduced to ten days and later trimmed to a staggering six. The riders were also a good source of news, spreading it far more quickly than by any other means available.

But financially the Pony Express was a disaster. Russell, Majors and Waddell were losing money hand over fist for one simple reason: their service cost far more to run than they could charge people for delivery! By the time the Pony Express had delivered its

---

* Against outlaws as well as Native Americans

final – and 34,753rd – item of mail,* the three partners were horribly in debt.

There was also the matter of the competition: the newly completed transcontinental telegraph, linking California to the rest of the state. Now messages could be Morse-coded down the line in next to no time.

Business failure though the Pony Express was, it really helped to create the legend of America's 'Wild West' and its heroes.**

* On 26 October 1861
** Including the likes of Buffalo Bill, who'd become a Pony Express rider when he was just 14

Happy Monday!

Monday is not the first day of the week,
Sunday is.*

* So why Sunday is part of the weekend rather than
the week-beginning escapes me

A road by any other name

What is wrong with the following statement?

> *'I was driving along a road in the
> City of London when a duck flew
> into my windscreen!'*

Any idea?

Well, technically there are no roads in the City of London. There are thoroughfares, but none of them is called a road. There are certainly streets and lanes though. When the Farringdon Road enters the city, its name changes to Farringdon Street!*

* Which is a bit of a cheat
NOTE: By the way, I don't know how to drive.

115

A giant leap

In 1730, Irishman James Kirkland made the mistake of accepting the offer of a job as footman to the Prussian Ambassador to London, Baron Borck. He travelled with Borck to England and was taken to a Prussian ship moored in Portsmouth. Once on board, he was grabbed, bound and gagged. Why? Because James Kirkland was over seven feet tall and he'd just been press-ganged into the Potsdam Guards.

The Potsdam Guards were members of a unique regiment of giant soldiers who formed the royal guard of King Frederick William I of Prussia. The king himself was a small, penny-pinching man . . . but when it came to his guards, money was no object.

A number of very tall men across Europe were kidnapped and press-ganged in the way Kirkland had been. They found themselves dressed in fine blue uniforms, served excellent food and paid according to their height.*

* The taller the man, the higher his pay!**
** And the king made them look even taller by having each man wear a 45-centimetre-high Grenadier cap

But discipline was harsh. Desertion was punishable by death. No wonder few people volunteered to serve of their own free will.

The Prussian press-gangers would go to great lengths to find new recruits. One story goes that a Bavarian carpenter was asked by one of Frederick William's agents to make a wooden box long and wide enough to fit the carpenter himself. When the agent returned to collect the box, he claimed it wasn't as big as he'd ordered.

When the carpenter proved him wrong by climbing into it, the agent had his men quickly nail the box's lid shut and the whole thing sent to Prussia!

In 1740, the king died, leaving behind a regiment of 2,500 giants which had never gone to war. He hadn't wanted any of his 'Blue Boys' injured!

Words can never hurt me

Kaiser* Wilhelm II of Germany – one of Queen Victoria's many grandchildren – was keen to try to improve relations between Germany and Britain. He therefore jumped at the opportunity to give an interview to a Colonel Stuart-Wortley to be published in the *Daily Telegraph*. Because of his importance, the newspaper was happy for the kaiser to have a copy of the article before it was published, to see if he wanted to make any changes to the text.

The German constitution required Wilhelm to pass a copy to the German prime minister** for government approval. Unfortunately for the kaiser, the prime minister either didn't look at it himself*** or saw the opportunity for some mischief-making. Either way, he passed it on to a more junior official.****

This official claimed to be under the

* Emperor
** Prince Bernhard von Bulow
*** Which is what he later claimed
**** Reinhold Klehmet

impression that he was supposed to be tidying up grammar or any simple errors but was meant to leave the main content of the interview unchanged . . .

. . . the result being that the *Daily Telegraph* published a most extraordinary interview in which the rambling Kaiser Bill seemed to manage to insult the English, the French, the Russians, the Japanese and even the Germans themselves!

He starts by saying, 'You English are mad, mad, mad as March hares', and probably couldn't have made a more botched job of the whole thing if he'd tried.

There are those who believe that the prime minister knew exactly what he was doing by letting the interview go through uncensored. Perhaps he'd been playing politics.

Six years later, Britain and Germany were at war.

A little heart to heart

In a highly unscientific survey carried out by me, it seems that most people think that the human heart is over on the left-hand side of the chest and there are even some who think it's heart-shaped.

Dealing with the second part first, of course the heart is heart-shaped because whatever shape the heart is must be heart-shaped . . . so by 'heart-shaped' I mean like this: – as seen on Valentine's cards and other soppy stuff. The heart is, in fact, much more the shape shown here.

As for being on the left-hand side of the chest, yes, it is more to the left than the right, but much nearer the middle than most people imagine.

So now you know.

High flyers

The Montgolfier brothers, who in the late 18th century built the first hot-air balloon to carry people, thought they'd discovered a brand-new gas that made balloons rise up into the air. They were wrong. In fact, it was just hot air (as in 'hot air rises').*

In 2008, a British Airways aeroplane was forced to make an emergency landing, resulting in dramatic pictures broadcast across the world. The media heaped praise on Captain Peter Burkhill. The only problem was that the man who actually landed the plane turned out not to have been him, but his co-pilot, First Officer John Coward, who, despite the name, certainly wasn't one. In the end, the praise was shared all round!

* You probably worked that out from the name 'hot-air balloon'

What's in a name?

Many people think that those well-known characters Bugs Bunny and Brer Rabbit are rabbits.* In truth, they're American jackrabbits – all one word – which are hares, not rabbits.

* An easy mistake to make when you consider their names!

Me and my big mouth

Oliver Locker-Lampson, British member of parliament from 1910 to 1945, once remarked that no MP could ever be arrested. Unfortunately for him, practical joker Horace de Vere Cole* overheard him say it . . . and planned to prove him wrong.

Horace de Vere Cole promptly challenged Oliver Locker-Lampson to run a race down a London Street. He accepted and the MP was soon streaking ahead. He was somewhat surprised when de Vere Cole started shouting, 'Stop thief!' and the police were soon after him too.

With nothing to hide, he stopped, and de Vere Cole told the police that this man had stolen his gold pocket watch. Sure enough, when Locker-Lampson's pockets were searched the watch was found on him (and he admitted that it wasn't his). The MP was promptly

* Most famous for tricking the navy into thinking that he and his friends were a bunch of Abyssinians and being given a tour around the battleship the HMS *Dreadnought*

arrested and taken into custody.

Only then did Horace de Vere Cole admit that he'd slipped his watch into the unsuspecting man's pocket to prove the MP wrong about something he'd said. Now *he* ended up being arrested too.

Not such a tower of strength

Fontill Abbey near Bath was one of the most impressive examples of a 'Gothic revival' building in Britain.* Built for wealthy eccentric William Thomas Beckford by architect James Wyatt at the turn of the 19th century, it included a 92-metre octagonal tower, making Fonthill Abbey the tallest private building in the whole of Europe at the time. Unfortunately, the tower fell down during construction. It was rebuilt . . . but then fell down again.

Beckford had 500 labourers working on the house day and night. He also got help from a further 450 men who'd been working at nearby Windsor Castle (and hurried up and finished there because he'd promised them ale).

Debts forced Beckford to sell the completed

* Gothic revival buildings were built in a loose interpretation of the medieval style (common in castles and churches)

building some years later. Sadly, the tower fell down for a THIRD time in 1825 and this time the rest of the building was eventually pulled down.*

* It was always thought that the tower kept on collapsing because the foundations hadn't been made strong enough or deep enough. A Channel Four TV documentary proved this wasn't true. Using radar, they discovered that proper foundations went right down to the bedrock

Does not compute!

In 1973, a US judge made a ruling that the world's first programmable all-electric computer had been completed in 1942/43 and made by an American by the name of Atanasoff. This was as part of a judgement in a legal case over a patent.

This was, in fact, a mistake. The world's first computer, Colossus, had been completed in 1941 by English telephone engineer Tommy Flowers (who spent much of his own money on its development). The reason why the judge knew nothing about it was because of the Official Secrets Act. The computer had been developed in top secret at Bletchley Park in Woking as part of efforts to crack German coded messages during the Second World War.*

The truth only came to light when a book was published in 1974, breaking the silence and revealing the incredible true story.

* The project was led by the brilliant all-round brainbox Alan Turing

Built in the days long before microchips, Colossus was very large and used valves which got very hot, making the room it was housed in very popular in winter and unpopular in the summer. It also made the computer room an ideal place for drying clothes.

After the war, Mr Flowers went back to working on telephone research, unable to tell anyone of his amazing achievement until many years later.*

* He died in 1998

Horseplay

When Henry VIII – of six-wives fame – was considering making Anne of Cleves wife number four, he wanted to get an idea what she looked like. Because she lived on the Continent, the king ordered her portrait be painted and delivered to him. He liked the portrait, so agreed to marry her. When they finally met in England, he was horrified by what he saw. As with most portraits of the time, the artist* had chosen to flatter his sitter. In Henry's eyes, Anne wasn't nearly as pretty in real life. He'd been duped!

It was too late for the king to cancel the wedding – there was too much at stake – but they soon divorced. Henry and Anne, however, remained on excellent terms . . . which was lucky when you consider that she'd earned the nickname 'the Flanders Mare',** and that he ultimately had two of his six wives beheaded.***

* A famous chap called Hans Holbein the Younger
** As in 'horse from Flanders'!
*** Anne got a palace, a castle and a manor house (including the furniture), plus an annual allowance and the official title of 'the king's beloved sister'

Feeeeeeling st-st-strange

Scottish surgeon James Simpson heard about
something called chloroform,* which he
thought might be useful for making operations less frightening and painful for his patients. In 1847, he decided to try it, to see if it
had any nasty side effects. Just in case things
went wrong, he wasn't sure who to use as
human guinea pigs . . . so he settled on himself and two other doctors, Dr Duncan and Dr
Keith (who were kind enough** to volunteer).

Once they'd been administered the chloroform,
all three men slumped to the floor in a deep
sleep. While Dr Duncan and Dr Keith lay stock-
still as they slept soundly, Simpson himself kept
waving his arms about and kicking the bottom
of a table he'd rolled under. Yup, they hadn't
even moved the furniture!

Feeling a little battered and bruised, Simpson
later declared the whole thing a big success.***

* An anaesthetic drug created by Samuel Guthrie
** Or crazy enough
*** And, ill-planned though the 'experiment' was,
Simpson was right. In 1853, Queen Victoria had
chloroform when giving birth to her eighth child

All at sea

When is a howler not a howler? When the people saying it's a howler are making a howler themselves. In his play *The Winter's Tale* William Shakespeare* famously refers to the shoreline of Bohemia. Over the centuries people have smugly pointed out that Bohemia is a landlocked country – surrounded by other countries – with no access to the sea.

In fact, not only did Bohemia stretch to the Adriatic Sea under the rule of King Premysl Ottocar II (1253–1278), but in 1526 the Kingdom of Bohemia included the Archduchy of Austria, which then included an Adriatic shoreline . . . but that doesn't stop people continuing to point out Shakespeare's so-called blunder.

* The world's greatest playwright of all time

Hard cheese

To think that ships can only fight battles on water and that cannons can only fire shells or cannonballs is certainly untrue. Just a few years after the American Civil War the US gunboat *Arakwe* was sent to the Horn of Aconcagua in the waters off Chile at the request of the Chilean government, who feared revolution. It was hoped that the sight of an American 'warship' might quell all thoughts of uprising. WRONG. For more than a year the ship patrolled the waters, and the rumblings of unrest continued on the land.

Just as Captain Alexander and his crew were making preparations to return home – following orders from the US government – there was an earthquake, swiftly followed by a tidal wave. The *Arakwe* was picked up and carried more than TWO MILES inland by the wave before being dumped unceremoniously on Chilean soil.

Fortunately for the crew, the boat was flat-bottomed and landed the right way up. No one was killed. All about them lay the wrecks of other grounded wooden vessels. These soon attracted looters: people who wanted to steal anything they could lay their hands on . . . and they eyed the *Arakwe* with interest too.

Fearing attack, Captain Alexander needed to find a way to keep the looters at bay. He was reluctant to fire at unarmed civilians but, when crowds gathered and prepared to board, he knew he must do something and ordered the firing of the cannons. This presented another problem. Despite having plenty of gunpowder, the crew couldn't reach the ammunition in the damaged ship: it was buried somewhere below decks.

The solution was a remarkable one: to fire the big round cheeses stored in the ship's galley! These were quickly loaded into the cannons with the gunpowder and were ready for firing!

Soon cannonball-sized cheeses were hurtling into the mob, eventually causing the looters to scatter and to flee. The *Arakwe* was down but not out.*

* The ship was subsequently officially recorded as being 'lost in action' and never put to sea again, but what a way to go!**
** And what a satisfying use of balls of cheese

Putting a foot in it

In 1962, Nikita Khrushchev, president of the USSR,* referred to China's revered leader Chairman Mao** as 'an old boot'. If that weren't bad enough, the Chinese word for 'boot' also means something EVEN MORE RUDE.*** Though both were communist, relations soon took a turn for the worse . . .

* Russia's 'Soviet Union'
** aka Mao Zedong
*** No, I'm not going to tell you what

Left? Right? Left?

A most unfortunate naval blunder occurred in 1893 off the coast of Lebanon, which resulted in the death of the commander of the British Mediterranean Fleet and 357 of his men. Tragically, this wasn't even during a sea battle but simply during manoeuvres.*

HMS *Victoria*** and HMS *Camperdown*** ended up colliding with each other and the *Victoria* sinking with all hands lost, including Vice-Admiral Sir George Tryon.

At a subsequent naval board a theory was put forward that Sir George had become confused between having the ship turn 180° and 90° when giving out orders!

* Practising moves!
** Not to be confused with Nelson's ship HMS *Victory*
*** Not to be confused with a camper van

May the Force be with you

The *Star Wars* films franchise is probably the most successful in the history of Hollywood. The merchandising of everything from *Star Wars* action figures to duvet covers is already way past $3,000,000,000 and rising . . .

. . . which is probably a teeny-weeny little bit upsetting for the 20th Century Fox rights executive who signed over all these rights to the director of *Star Wars*, George Lucas, before the first *Star Wars* film had even been released.

I bet they won't make that mistake again!

Mistaken identity

Once an animal has been classified and named it can't be called something else or things might get confusing. That's why there's no such thing as a brontosaurus. It turns out that the dinosaur named brontosaurus was actually the same dinosaur as the apatosaurus* so, since the 1970s, the name brontosaurus has been dropped.

* Funnily enough, the name 'apatosaurus' means 'deceptive lizard'. No wonder it was fooling people!

A BIG mistake

In the 1988 film *Big* starring Tom Hanks,
Hanks plays a boy who grows into an adult
overnight. In one scene he goes home and
tries to convince his mother that he really is
her son, just somehow grown-up. In an effort
to make her believe him, he tells her that his
birthday is 3 November.

This is all well and good, except that in a later
scene we see a milk carton* with a photo of
the Tom Hanks character, reported 'missing' as
a young boy, and his date of birth as being in
January!**

* In 1980s America, milk cartons had faces of missing
children and information about them printed on the
side, with headlines along the lines of: 'Have you seen
me?' Over 1,400 children were found as a direct result
of this ingenious campaign.

** No wonder she didn't believe him!

The world's most famous stamp?

Rummaging through the attic in his home in 1873, 12-year-old Scottish boy Vernon Vaughan found some old stamps. Among these was a magenta-coloured one from British Guiana, marked '1 cent', stuck to an envelope.

Unaware of its true value, Vaughan sold the stamp to a local collector, N. R. McKinnon, for six shillings,* which was, I'll admit, better than a slap in the face with sun-warmed kipper but (with hindsight) a mistake.

In the 1900s, after being sold a few more times, it fell into the hands of one of the world's most famous stamp collectors, a man with the very impressive name of Count Philippe de la Renotiere von Ferrari, who paid £150 for it. He had realized that it was INCREDIBLY RARE.

Back in 1856, British Guiana had run out of stamps so the firm of Joseph Baum 👉

* 30p, but back when 30p would buy a whole lot more than today

and William Dallas, publishers of the *Official Gazette* in Georgetown, were granted permission to print an emergency issue until a new batch arrived from England. The newspaper's four-cent stamp was well known . . . but this was a one-cent: the only one-cent stamp known to be in existence. It was indescribably exciting for a true collector to own such a thing!

The count kept the stamp until his death in 1917. When he died, the French government seized his property. The count had taken German citizenship and the French were at war with Germany.

In 1922 – the First World War having ended in 1918 – the French put the 1856 one-cent British Guiana 'Black on Magenta' up for auction. Those bidding for the stamp included a representative of Britain's King George V.

In the end, it turned into a bidding war between American millionaires Maurice Burrus and Arthur Hind. Hind won, getting the stamp for what was then a staggering £7,343.*

But the story doesn't end there. After Hind died, his wife claimed that she'd been left that one particular stamp, and she sold it. It didn't resurface until 1970 when it was sold one last time. Today the 1856 one-cent British Guiana 'Black on Magenta' has been valued at around $1 million dollars.

There is one thing that has puzzled some people though. Vernon Vaughan had said that he'd found the stamp on an envelope. But it cost four cents to send a letter. One cent would have only covered the postage for a newspaper.

You don't think? Surely not? If someone had somehow tampered with a four-cent stamp to make it appear like a unique one-cent stamp, the experts would have noticed.

Wouldn't they?

* Back when £7,343 was big bucks

Please hold . . .

In October 2007, aeroplanes were left circling the skies in a holding pattern above Athens airport when one of their air traffic controllers failed to show up for work. They didn't have anyone immediately to hand to take his place!

To bee or not to bee?

We've all heard the 'fact' that bumblebees can't fly; that it's 'aerodynamically impossible' and 'against the laws of physics and/or nature', and it only succeeds 'under the power of its own ignorance'.

This is obviously NOT TRUE because – er – bumblebees do fly and there's no such thing as real magic . . . so where on earth does this mistakery come from?

The answer probably lies between the covers of a book called *Le Vol des Insectes* by Antoine Magan, published in 1934. In it Magan discusses a mathematical equation formulated by an engineer named André Sainte-Laguë. The equation proves that it wouldn't be possible for something travelling at the speed of a bumblebee to achieve the maximum lift for an aircraft's wings.*

Although this isn't the same as saying that a bumblebee – which, remember,

* To put its simply: an aeroplane the size of a bumblebee, moving as slowly as a bumblebee, couldn't fly

doesn't have the fixed/stationary wings of an aeroplane – shouldn't be able to fly, the idea that this was what the book was saying captured the imagination and soon spread. An urban myth was born.

Of course, aerodynamic equations explaining aeroplane flight are based on steady-wing and not mobile-wing movement. The fact that a fixed-wing aeroplane the size, shape and speed of a bumblebee couldn't fly has nothing to do with the fantastically complicated functions of an insect's moving wings.

A small matter of trust

The early nation of Scotland was made up of five different peoples: the Scots (who originally came from Ireland), the Picts,* the Celtic Britons, the Angles** and the invading Vikings.***

In AD 843, the Picts and the Scots mistrusted each other in a BIG way . . . but their greater fear of the Viking invaders led to the possibility of their becoming uneasy allies.

According to legend, the Pictish princes and nobles received an invitation from Scottish king Kenneth MacAlpin of Dalriada to come to Scone. There, he declared, they would agree upon one man to rule both the picts of Caledonia and Scottish Dalriada.

The Picts' blunder was to take him as a man of his word, which was a bad move. Definitely a *very* bad move.

* Which means 'painted men'
** aka the English
*** Who originally inhabited much of Scotland, then eventually settled for 'the Kingdom of the isles'

When they arrived in Scone, the Picts met the Scottish representatives in a muddy field, in the centre of which was a raised wooden 'conference platform' where, apparently, the leaders of both sides could talk and be seen and heard.

What the Picts didn't realize – until it was too late – was what a terrible mistake they'd made coming there. Once they were on the platform, the Scots pulled out a support, causing the platform to collapse and those on it to fall into a large pit hidden beneath.

King Kenneth's men slaughtered them all before they had chance to scramble out. This betrayal became known as the Treachery of Scone and made King Kenneth ruler of a whole area called Alban (from which later grew the Scotland we know today), which is why we never hear much about the Picts. . .

. . . or so the legend goes. Historians now believe that the Treachery of Scone is a story rather than fact, but an ancient story passed down the generations, with its own place in Scottish history.

A matter of safety

Garry Hoy, a lawyer with Canadian law firm Holden Day Wilson, regularly demonstrated to visiting law students the strength of the safety glass in the windows of their offices in a Toronto skyscraper by throwing himself at one. However, it's thought that he used the same window on each occasion and, over time, the glass must have weakened. One day, he ran at the glass and crashed straight through it, falling 24 storeys to his death in the courtyard below.

Dishing the dirt

As recently as 200 years ago, hospitals made a number of very basic blunders when it came to trying to keep their patients alive. If you were due to have a limb amputated, you might hope to see your surgeon wearing a very bloody apron to show just how many similar operations he'd already performed. (No one wants a first-timer sawing off their leg!)

Surgeons also prided themselves on their speed. Surely the sooner you hacked and sawed a limb off, the better the chance of survival? (Well, no, actually, but isn't hindsight* a wonderful thing?)

It didn't occur to anyone that it might be an idea to wash the surgical implements – saws, etc. – between procedures either. It was the same with sheets on the beds. What was the point of washing and changing them between patients? They'd only get dirty again.

---

* Looking back at something with the benefit of information obtained after the event

And none of the staff ever washed their hands.*

Today these seem such obvious boo-boos, but it's worth remembering that back then nobody knew about GERMS. We do, which is why we see things so differently.

---

* It wasn't until 1847 that Hungarian doctor Ignaz Semmelweis came up with this suggestion – before and after delivering babies – saving numerous lives

Doing a Ratner

Ratner's used to be the largest jewellery retailer in the world. In 1991, it had 2,500 shops, around 27,000 staff, billions of pounds a year turnover and profits of £125 million.

This was the year that its boss, Gerald Ratner, gave a speech to the Institute of Directors in which he said, among other things, that his shops 'sell a pair of earrings for under a pound, which is cheaper than a prawn sandwich from Marks & Spencer. But I have to say the earrings probably wouldn't last as long'.

His comments were widely reported in the press, and former customers of Ratner's – who didn't like being taken for mugs – stopped shopping at the stores.

An estimated £500 million is thought to have been wiped off the company's value, which eventually dropped the Ratner's name in an effort to recover. Ratner himself lost his job and his £650,000-a-year salary.

As a result, putting your foot in your mouth

in such a big way is still sometimes referred to as 'doing a Ratner'.*

---

* There is, however, a happy ending for Gerald Ratner. Since then, he's built up the largest online jewellery store in the UK. He's a dot.com millionaire

Say what you really think

During elections in Ontario, Canada, in 2003, one of the parties described the leader of another party in a press release as being 'an evil reptilian kitten-eater from another planet'. When this caused outrage, party officials argued that it had been meant as a joke. No one would really think that the man was an evil reptilian kitten-eater from another planet (or even from Earth, come to that). This did them no good though, and their credibility was badly dented.*

* And the so-called evil reptilian kitten-eater's party won. They celebrated with a big bowl of kitten stew**
** NO! NOT TRUE! I made that last part up

With friends like these . . .

In 1788, the Austrian forces of Emperor Joseph planned attacks on the Turks in Transylvania. Things started badly with around 170,000 Austrian troops catching malaria from which around 33,000 subsequently died. But their troubles didn't end there. Emperor Joseph took half his forces to face the Turkish Grand Vizier near the town of Karánsebes . . .

. . . Unfortunately, some of the foot soldiers managed to buy alcohol from locals along the way. The officers told them off, which caused the foot soldiers to get angry and rather rowdy. To panic the officers, some of the soldiers* started shouting that the Turks were attacking!

Soon matters got out of hand, with just about everyone thinking that everyone else was the enemy and shooting at each other.

By morning, 10,000 Austrians lay dead, each killed by his own side. The Turks were still miles away.

* Who'd probably already had a bit too much to drink

'The hags flung out . . .'

William Archibald Spooner* (1844–1930) gave his name to spoonerisms, the unintentional swapping of the beginning of one word for that of another** so, for example, 'We'll have the flags hung out' becomes 'We'll have the hags flung out'. In fact, most of the spoonerisms attributed to him were either deliberately or accidentally spoken by other people. The most famous include:

'You have hissed all my mystery lectures, and were caught fighting a liar in the quad. Having tasted two worms, you will leave by the next town drain.' ('You have missed all my history lectures, and were caught lighting a fire in the quad. Having wasted two terms, you will leave by the next down train.')

'A well-boiled icicle' ('A well-oiled bicycle')

* Spooner was at Oxford University as an undergraduate, fellow, lecturer, tutor, Dean and, finally, Warden. He was well-liked and well-respected
** Called transposition. The first recorded transposition in English appears in Henry Pelham's *The Complete Gentleman* of 1622, where 'Sir, I must go buy a dagger' becomes 'Sir, I must go dye a beggar.'

'Is the bean dizzy?' ('Is the dean busy?')

 'Go and shake a tower.' ('Go and take a shower.')

 'Come into the arms of the shoving leopard' ('Come into the arms of the loving shepherd.')

A major hiccup

In 1872, the *Royal Adelaide*,* a cargo ship, ran aground on the treacherous Chesil Beach in Dorset.** Six sailors were killed. Twenty locals also died as a result of the wreck.

They weren't hit by the ship. They didn't drown when attempting any kind of rescue. What they did do was salvage some of the washed-up cargo – which turned out to be alcohol – and drink it. Far too much of it, by all accounts. They went from being dead drunk to just plain dead.

* Not to be confused with the steam ship of the same name that was wrecked in 1849
** Near where the swannery is today***
*** And if you don't know what a swannery is, have a wild guess (not a wild goose****)
**** Though the answer *is* bird-related

A stunt too far

US stuntman John Barras's attempt to be 'buried alive' tragically resulted in his death. In a glare of publicity in Fresno, California, Barras was bound in chains and put in a clear perspex coffin which was then lowered into a hole in the ground.

Soil was then placed on top, followed by wet cement, which was when things didn't go according to plan. The weight of the cement caused the lid of the coffin to break and the liquid poured in, killing him.

The whole event was captured on film.

Stamping his name on it

The first postage stamp in the world was the (British) Penny Black, which is why it doesn't have the country of issue on it.* On it was a picture of Queen Victoria's head and the words: POSTAGE ONE PENNY. This was the brainchild of Rowland Hill, which is why people often make the mistake of assuming that he invented the stick-on stamp.

Rowland Hill had come up with the idea for a penny post but couldn't think of how it might work, so in 1839 a public competition was announced. The prize was £200, and over 2,600 people entered their suggestions. None of them seemed quite right to Hill, so he took various elements people had suggested – along with his own ideas – and came up with the Penny Black.

One of the entrants had been a bookseller from Dundee in Scotland by the name of James Chalmers. Although he hadn't won the £200, he had entered the suggestion of a

* Think about it: where else could they be from?

stick-on stamp. When, on 6 May 1840, the first Penny Black went on sale, the world recognized Rowland Hill as the inventor of the postage stamp . . . and Chalmers probably felt a bit miffed, and rightly so.

PS The biggest mistake with the Penny Black, however, was the fact that it was black. This meant that the postmark had to be franked with red ink, which was expensive. In 1841, the stamps were changed to Penny Reds and the stamps were franked in black!

Taking it on the chin

John L. Sullivan, an imposing figure, was boxing's World Heavyweight Champion from 1882 to 1892 and had never been knocked out in his life, in or out of competition. On a number of occasions, Sullivan gave boxing exhibitions around Britain. As a novelty attraction, he agreed to spar with Hessie Donahue, a woman who ran a boxing school. You guessed it. Big mistake.*

Donahue got in a lucky punch and knocked him senseless. Apparently he was never knocked out again. That was the one and only time.**

* With hindsight, of course
** I wonder whether it was the last time he sparred with a woman too?

Going out with a bang

William Bent built a series of forts on America's Santa Fe trail, but usually ended up destroying them himself! Bent was very keen to live in peace with anyone and everyone and his stockades were more trading posts, built for protection should it be needed.

He destroyed his first fort not long after its grand opening. At the opening event there were three days of feasting and celebrations involving locals including Mexicans and Cheyenne Native Americans . . . followed by an outbreak of smallpox.

When the Cheyennes started dying in their homes outside the stockade, Bent had them brought into it to be cared for by him and his men. Once the last of the dead was buried, Bent burned down the fort.

But William Bent didn't give up! He built a second wooden fort and this time a truce between the various Native American tribes meant that this opening was an even grander opening than the last one . . . and this time people started dying of cholera. And this fort had to be burned down by Bent too.

Bent's third fort was built out of adobe*
and survived the aftermath of its opening
celebrations.** When war broke out with
Mexico, the US government used this fort as
an army supply base. When the war ended,
Bent was told that, as it had been used by the
US army once, the US government could take
over his fort again any time they needed it.

They were forgetting that here was a man with
experience of destroying his own forts! There
was no way Bent was going to let anyone
commandeer HIS property.

Bent couldn't burn it down because it wasn't
made of logs, as the previous two forts had
been. But that didn't stop him. Instead, he
packed the place with kegs of gunpowder and
then – BOOM! – blew it sky high!

* Mud bricks
** Perhaps sensible people were staying away from
them by now. An invitation to an opening of one of
Bill Bent's forts might have a kiss of death about it!

It came from beneath the waves . . .

The Sargasso Sea* once had the reputation of being a 'ship graveyard', with so many vessels being wrecked there. It was believed that the culprit was seaweed. Yes, you read that correctly: SEAWEED. The particular villain of the piece was thought to be the Pacific giant kelp, which grows up to 60 metres long. It was imagined that ships somehow became entangled in it and pulled under. This later proved to be piffle.**

* In the North Atlantic
** As in 'really not so'

Listen 'ere

When French doctor René-Théophile-
Hyacinthe Laennec invented the stethoscope
in 1816,* many people were unimpressed and
some even mocked. This was hardly surprising
when you consider that it was just a piece
of cardboard rolled into a cylinder and held
to the patient's chest. On the other hand, it
was ingenious in its simplicity, and modern
stethoscopes are simply a refinement of the
idea.

* And wrote about it in 1819

A message misunderstood

On 30 March 1944, the Allied forces in the Second World War lost 96 bombers. One of the Allied bombers up in the air that night was a Halifax piloted by Captain Cyril Barton with a six-man crew. With 70 miles still to fly to Nuremberg (the target for their bombs), their intercom system – for communicating between crew members – was put out of action by enemy fire, as were the plane's machine guns.

Without the intercom, three members of the crew misunderstood an instruction, a blunder which caused them to bail out – in other words parachute from the plane – leaving the remaining men without a wireless operator,* a navigator** and a bomb-aimer.*** Despite this unfortunate error, the four remaining men reached Nuremberg and dropped the bombs . . .

Now all they had to do was get home ☞

* To keep in touch with base
** To tell them where they were and where to go
*** You can work that one out for yourself

in one piece. Against all the odds, Captain Barton got the Halifax and his three remaining crew back to England. Flying with just one engine, he managed to steer the stricken plane away from some houses before crash-landing. Barton's three remaining crew members all survived, as did those who'd parachuted out by mistake.* Captain Barton himself was killed. He was awarded a posthumous** Victoria Cross.

* And been captured
** After death

Baffling blunders, and oh-so unfair

Under other circumstances, Lord Cochrane might be remembered today as one of England's great sea heroes. As it is – if he's remembered for anything – it's usually for one big cock-up which wasn't even his fault.

His most successful year was probably 1801 when, captaining a little brig called *Speedy*,* he managed to capture more than fifty Spanish and French vessels during a number of different naval engagements. On one occasion, he'd boarded a huge Spanish frigate, with his crew's faces blackened to scare the living daylights out of the enemy.

Later, when captaining the *Imperieuse*, he kept on raiding the Spanish coast, blowing up coastal roads and blowing them up again just as soon as they'd been repaired. This way, the enemy were always kept busy and unable to attack the British. And how did the British Admiralty reward such an ingenious

* Which wasn't

strategy? By issuing Cochrane with an official reprimand for using more equipment – from gunpowder to sails – than any other captain afloat!

Then came Cochrane's big opportunity. Another admiral – Lord Gambier – was in charge of blockading the French fleet. There were fears that the French might soon break through the blockade and escape, so the Admiralty wanted the French ships destroyed.

Unfortunately, Gambier had either become more laid-back in his old age or possibly – dare I say it? – gone a little gaga. When ordered to attack the French with fireships,* he said that they were 'a horrible and unchristian mode of warfare'** and began handing out religious pamphlets to his crew!

Now that he was there, Cochrane planned to attack the enemy fleet. He had three vessels filled with 1,500 kegs of gunpowder each, held together with rope, to make three floating

* Unmanned ships set ablaze and sent into the enemy fleet in the hope of setting its (wooden) ships alight
** Which it was, but it was naval practice at the time and he was an admiral, remember!

bombs. On top of these were placed hundreds of hand grenades and live shells. He wanted to do some SERIOUS damage and to cause real panic.

Now came the cunning plan. If, once the three floating bombs had exploded, fireships were sent towards the fleet, then the French might think that they too were enormous bombs. One way to tackle a fireship was to board it and steer it away from your ships . . . but no one would be foolish enough to board a vessel that might be another massive BOMB.

When night fell and it was time to attack, the weather conditions were stormy. Cochrane himself was aboard the first bomb, with an officer and four sailors, as it floated towards the enemy. It was he who lit the fuse and jumped into the attached rowing boat, where the others nervously waited. The fuse was supposed to take 12 minutes to burn. It only took five.

By the end of the attack, the ships of the French blockade had separated from each other and most of them ended up lying helpless on shore. Cochrane's plan might not have destroyed them outright, but now – the following morning – all the British fleet had to do was to move in for the kill.

When Cochrane sent urgent signals to Gambier to send in the British ships, Gambier simply acknowledged having received them but did nothing more!!!

In the end, Lord Cochrane attacked three French ships with his single frigate. This caused Gambier to do something at last, firing constantly on the stranded French vessels . . . until nightfall when, without orders to do so, he simply stopped. When Cochrane declared that he was going to attack again at dawn with the aid of five brigs, Gambier recalled him.

In an extraordinary turn of events, the British authorities made a blunder of their own. It was later announced that there would be a vote of thanks for Admiral Gambier* in the House of Commons for his actions against the French. Cochrane – who was an MP – made it known that he would oppose the motion. Gambier then demanded that, if he had done

* Yup, Gambier, not Cochrane.

something wrong, he – Gambier – should be court-martialled, which he was.

When – surprise, surprise – Gambier received 'an honourable acquittal', the vote of thanks went ahead and it was Cochrane whose reputation was in tatters. He resigned from the British navy.*

* But he was a big hit with the Chilean and Brazilian navies, and went on to do them proud

Nothing but hot air

When the Montolfier brothers launched their first hot-air balloon flights over Paris, some people living in the countryside – who'd heard nothing about this seemingly magical new mode of transport – were thrown into a state of panic.

Learning from this mistake, the French government issued a warning notice in 1783 – spread far and wide – which proclaimed:

Anyone seeing a sky globe similar to
the obscured moon must know that, far
from being a frightening phenomenon,
it is a machine made of taffeta and light
cloth which is absolutely harmless and
will be of great help to society some day.

Now you see them . . .

The first English colony in North America was founded in 1583 in an 800-mile area of Newfoundland, claimed for England. The expedition was led by Sir Walter Raleigh's half-brother Sir Humphrey Gilbert. Unfortunately, the colonists became sick and disgruntled and decided to leave.

They set sail for home, but their ship sank and they all drowned.

The second colony was set up in 1585 on the island of Roanoke, off what is now the coast of North Carolina. It was named Virginia after Elizabeth, the Virgin Queen.* Although Sir Walter was put in charge of the region, he didn't go along. The 107 colonists were taken out in seven ships under the command of Sir Richard Grenville.

When Grenville returned home, the colony fell apart. They were short of food and then a hurricane headed their way. Fortunately for

---

* Not to be confused with the state of Virginia, which came into being much later elsewhere

them, they hitched a lift back to England with none other than Sir Francis Drake.

A few days later, a ship full of supplies sent by Sir Walter Raleigh arrived in Roanoke to find the place deserted. The whole series of events seemed to be turning into a well-orchestrated farce!

Two weeks later, Sir Richard Grenville was back and equally surprised to find the colony gone. To make sure that there was still an English presence in the area – claiming it as English soil – he left behind 15 of his own men with enough supplies to last them two years.

Sir Walter, meanwhile, sent out yet ANOTHER group of colonists from Portsmouth in 1587. This time their number included 17 women and nine children. They were under the leadership of Governor John White.

On arrival, they expected to be greeted by Sir Richard Grenville's men. Instead, they found a single skeleton.* They never found hide nor hair of the other 14 men.

* All that was left of a man who appeared to have been murdered

White's colonists did their best to settle in, and on 18 August 1587 White's daughter, Eleanor Dare, gave birth to the first child of English parents to be born in America. They called her Virginia.

Just a few days later, Governor White and some of the settlers set sail for England to get supplies, planning to be back by spring. In fact, it was two years before they returned.*

Two rowing boats were sent ashore. One overturned in rough waters, drowning seven men. This was yet another disaster in a catalogue of disasters.

When White reached the colony he found it

* England had other things to deal with, such as the Spanish Armada.

empty. There was no one there. The colonists had vanished, never to be seen again. England's attempts at colonizing America appear to have been jinxed from the outset.

To boldly go

Robert O'Hara Burke, an Irish ex-soldier and Melbourne police officer, and William J. Wills of the Melbourne Observatory joined forces in order to take up the challenge of trying to win a cash prize and 1,000 acres of land rent free for seven years. The year was 1860. The country was Australia. The prize was for being the first to travel from the south coast to the north coast and back again: a journey of around 3,600 miles.

Neither Burke nor Wills had any experience of such expeditions and neither did their men.

They set off in August of that year with 24 camels and 23 horse-drawn wagons.* Progress was so slow that Burke and Wills split away from the main expedition taking two men, Charles Gray and John King, with them.

* Or 26 or 27 camels** and 28 horse-drawn wagons, depending on who you choose to believe
** The expedition set off with 60 gallons of rum for the camels – yes, *the camels* – but the men started drinking it – hic! – too. When Burke found out he flew into a terrible rage and, much to the men's dismay, made them leave (what was left of) it behind!

Amazingly, Burke's small group made it to the north coast, on 11 February 1861. On the way back though, Charles Gray died. When the remaining three returned to Cooper's Creek, where the main expedition was supposed to be waiting for them, they found a note saying that their supplies were low, they assumed Burke, Wills and the others dead, and they were heading for home.

Unfortunately, instead of heading out after them, Burke, Wills and King made the extraordinarily misguided decision to go another way. They got lost, ate their camels, then found their way back to Cooper's Creek again. Here Burke died on 30 June 1861 and Wills soon after.

John King survived, purely thanks to some Aborigine people who found him by chance and nursed him back to health. On 15 September 1861 he was rescued.

Burke and Wills's bodies were taken back to Melbourne for a state funeral.

Practice makes perfect

During a rugby match between Harlequins and Gloucester in October 1969, Harlequin player Bob Hiller missed ELEVEN goal kicks. He was so frustrated by his efforts that he stayed on the pitch when the match was over to keep practising.*

* And much of the crowd stayed behind too, to watch

A blaze of excitement

When one end of London Bridge caught fire in
1212 it caused such excitement that thousands
of people came to have a closer look, many
of them swarming on to the bridge itself.
When the wind suddenly changed direction,
sparks flew from one end to the other, so soon
both ends were alight with hordes of people
trapped in the middle. Many of those who
weren't burned to death or trampled in the
panic were drowned when they jumped or fell
into the River Thames. By the end of the day,
over 3,000 people had been killed.

Germany calling!

William Joyce made a number of mistakes in his life. Here are just four of them:

1. Joyce's father had been Irish and his mother English, but he'd been born in New York. His father took American citizenship but, in the 1930s, Joyce applied for a British passport and was granted one.

2. Having become a fascist, he moved to Germany and during the Second World War, broadcast from there under the name Lord Haw Haw, beginning each broadcast with, 'Germany calling . . . Germany calling . . .' then spreading Nazi propaganda.

3. When Germany surrendered and Joyce went on the run he was cocky enough to speak to a British officer near the Danish border. The man recognized his distinctive voice from the radio and ended up shooting him in the leg.

4. On trial at the Old Bailey in England 'Lord Haw Haw' misjudged the mood of the people and felt sure he'd be acquitted. Because he had a British passport it was decided that he

should stand trial for treason.

He was found guilty. The penalty was death.*

* He was hanged on 3 January 1946

Suckers!

Hubert Cecil Booth's electrically operated vacuum cleaner was a little on the large side. It was housed in a horse-drawn carriage which had to remain OUTSIDE the house.* The suction hoses leading from the machine had to be fed through open doors and windows, where the cleaning staff would then use them to clean carpets, curtains and, according to his literature, even tapestries. There was one problem though: it was so noisy that the horse would often bolt in fear, taking the vacuum-cleaner cart, and all its hoses, with it!

* It would have been tricky trying to keep it in the cupboard under the stairs

This will do

In 1535, Jacques Cartier sailed up the St Lawrence River* in the hope of finding a way to China. He didn't. Instead he discovered much of Canada** for the west.

* In those days called the Hochelaga River
** Canada was actually a Canadian Indian word just meaning 'town' or 'village'

187

A slight misunderstanding

The Russian word for railway station is pronounced 'voxzall', and this apparently came about due to a misunderstanding at the highest level.

When the Tsar of Russia visited England early in Queen Victoria's reign,* he passed Vauxhall railway station and asked what it was called. The British official accompanying him replied, 'Vauxhall.'

When the Tsar returned to Russia and ordered the construction of his own railway system, he said the stations should be called 'voxzall': a new word for a new kind of building.

* When Britain's steam-railway system was expanding

Hot stuff!

A college rugby match in Tonga turned out to have very expensive consequences. The match itself was straightforward enough, but the riot arising from the result led to the college itself being burnt to the ground. The damage was estimated to be around £480,000!

A tragic error and incredible courage

In 1665, London was at the mercy of the Great Plague.* At the time, no one knew what caused it, but people did know that it spread most quickly where there were many people living side by side, so those who could – usually the rich – left town. The king and his court relocated to the city of Oxford.

Those who lived deep in the countryside – particularly in isolated villages in remote regions – were far safer because, in fact, the plague was carried by fleas which, in turn, were often carried by black rats.

Tragically, one such isolated village did not escape the Great Plague's clutches. Someone in the Derbyshire village of Eyam** ordered some clothes – some new, some second-hand – from a London tailor. The tailor duly wrapped the clothes and had them delivered to the village in the late summer of that year.

* Which eventually killed around 65,000 Londoners
** Pronounced 'Eem'

This simple, innocent act was in fact a dreadful mistake. As with so many clothes of the day – long before detergents and endless supplies of hot water – the clothes contained fleas: fleas that carried the plague. By October, 25 people in the village had died.

It was then that the rector* of Eyam, William Mompesson, came up with a plan, which the villagers agreed to: to limit the possibility of their spreading the plague to other villages – even though they didn't know how it actually spread – they would cut themselves off from the outside world. No one would leave the village, and no one else would be allowed in.

They marked out a boundary around Eyam with stones and made arrangements that supplies would be left at agreed times on agreed days in agreed places on the boundary. To pay for these goods, they left money soaked in vinegar.**

This extraordinary act of courage worked, in that it did stop the spread of the ☞

* A clergyman
** Which they thought would somehow purify it

disease to their neighbours in the surrounding countryside, but at an incredible sacrifice to themselves. Over 259 villagers – more than two-thirds of the population of Eyam – had died. Their remarkable story, however, lives on.

A dollop of Trollope

Today, Anthony Trollope is rightly remembered as a world-class writer and – for those who enjoy unlikely-but-true facts – as the inventor of the pillar box* for the Post Office. For much of his life, however, he was simply seen as a rather unlikable grump.

Although Trollope lived in Ireland during the famine, he all but ignored the starvation going on around him because he was rich enough to have food on his own table.

He didn't know what the fuss was about for the anti-slavery abolitionists either. Apparently he thought slavery was a good idea. He also turned a blind eye to the horrors, dangers and poverty of industrialized Britain.

Later in life, Anthony Trollope decided to try his hand at politics. He was good at writing, wasn't he? So perhaps he could write and deliver stirring political speeches. Wrong. It was the general consensus that they were pretty terrible. When he stood for election he came last.

* Nowadays more commonly referred to as a postbox

A personal apology

This mistake was mine so probably doesn't belong in this book, but I feel guilty about it and including it here might help me feel better. Opposite the entrance to the National Portrait Gallery in London, just a few strides from the church of St Martin-in-the-Fields, is a statue to a woman which is more plinth – or block of stone – than it is actual statue of a woman.

I'd been passing that statue for years. I used to live in London and still visit it regularly enough and I'd always assumed that the statue was built to commemorate some worthy educator. There's nothing wrong with having been a worthy educator, but I thought the monument was a bit over the top for that. It's BIG.

Then, one day, I stopped and looked at
the statue – I can't remember why – and I
discovered that it was in memory of someone
called Edith Cavell. The name sounded
familiar but I couldn't place her. Then I
read the quotes around the base and was
determined to find out.

As a young woman, Edith Cavell nursed her
sick father and this made her decide to train
as a nurse. She was a matron in Manchester
when she was offered a post in Brussels,
Belgium, in 1907.

Cavell was still in Belgium when the First
World War broke out and German forces swept
through the country. Allied soldiers were
separated from their regiments and cut off
from them. Some were badly wounded. Cavell
not only tended these wounded in her hospital
but also helped them to get to the Dutch
border to escape. She helped over 200 men in
this way.

The actions of this well-to-do daughter of an
English country parson* soon came to ☞

* Another type of clergyman

the attention of the German occupying forces. Cavell was arrested, tricked into signing a confession and accused of being a British spy.

On 12 October 1915, she was shot by a firing squad. Although many countries were at war, this was seen as a particularly cowardly and uncivilized act. Protests came from governments around the world.

Today, Edith Cavell is not only commemorated by the monument opposite the National Portrait Gallery, her name is also given to the Edith Cavell Institute of Medicine and Surgery.

Her last recorded words were:

'I realize that patriotism is not enough. I must have no hatred or bitterness towards anyone . . . These men are sick, wounded and in need of help.'

These words are on her monument. Perhaps, in some way, she was an educator after all.

A stitch in time

When, in 46 BC, Julius Caesar's astronomers calculated that there were actually 365¼ days in a year and not 365, as in their existing Roman calendar, they too made a minor error that was to have a lasting effect. They got around the problem of the quarter day by making a normal year in the new Julian Calendar* 365 days long, and adding up the four quarters to make one whole extra day every four years.**

But, in reality, it takes 365 days, 5 hours, 48 minutes and 46-ish seconds for the Earth to travel one complete orbit around the sun . . . and this 11-minute difference was to have a lasting effect.

By 1752, this tiny difference had caused the Julian Calendar to be eleven DAYS out from the Earth's actual orbit. To correct this, countries which hadn't already adapted to Pope Gregory's*** Gregorian Calendar ☞

* Named Julian after Julius, geddit?
** Which is why leap years have 366 days
*** Whose astronomers had spotted the error and cut ten days

in 1582 had to 'lose eleven days'. Such countries included Britain and Russia, where outraged peasants are said to have demanded to be 'given back' their stolen days!

The reason why some countries had switched to the Gregorian Calendar some 170-or-so years before others was because of religion. The Catholic countries had followed their Pope's decrees, but by 1582 Britain had broken away to form its own church so would have nothing to do with this newfangled papist calender.

Pope Gregory's Gregorian Calendar had one more trick up its sleeve. It was necessary for 29 February – the extra day added in leap years – to be left OUT of the last leap year of each century unless the number could be divided by 400, in which case it stayed in.*

This way, the Earth's orbit and our calendar stay very much in sync.

* The year 2000 was the last year of the 20th century – even though some idiots thought 1999 was – and it was also the last leap year of the 20th century. It kept its 29 February, because 400 goes into 2000 a neat 5 times

As mad as hatters!

In the 1980s BBC TV comedy show *Not the Nine O'Clock News*, one sketch involved reports of a person having been arrested for wearing 'a loud shirt in a built-up area'. But fact is often stranger than fiction.

In 1797, the wearing of a newfangled HAT in Britain led to a genuine arrest. The hat's creator, John Hetherington, thought that sporting his 'tall-crowned beaver'* would attract admiring glances. Instead, it caused a riot, with outraged people chasing him down the street!

He ended up in court for 'having appeared on the public highway wearing upon his head a tall structure having a shining lustre calculated to frighten timid people'!**

* One of the first silk top hats, AND with glossy finish
** Don't you just love the idea of a hat frightening timid people?!

A terrible blunder

In October 1904, a fleet of trawlers from the English town of Hull was fishing in the North Sea* when it was attacked by Russian warships. The warships fired at the vessels for a quarter of an hour. Amazingly, only one trawler actually sank and only three men were killed, but more than fifty of them were seriously injured. The attack had been at night. Had it happened in daylight, the deaths and casualties might have been far worse.

Russia was not at war with Britain, and was ruled by the Tsar, who was supposedly a friend of Britain. There was outrage throughout Europe. Although the Tsar sent his 'regrets' about what had happened, he ignored all demands for some kind of inquiry as to WHY it had happened.

The protests became more urgent as other countries worried what the Imperial Russian naval fleet might do to their ships, but still the Tsar chose to ignore them.

* In an area called Dogger Bank

It was only when Britain ordered the Royal Navy to pursue all Russian vessels and to take 'such action as is necessary' to prevent anything like the attack at Dogger Bank happening again, that the Tsar finally acted. If he hadn't, war may well have broken out in Europe.

A Russian court of inquiry found that one of their secret service agents* had reported that their actual enemy, the Japanese – whom they were fighting in the Far East – were planning to attack the Russian fleet off Denmark. And this had been accepted as fact.

This was crazy, because the Japanese would have had to sail thousands of miles to make such an attack, which would have been no real advantage to them anyway. And they would probably have been spotted – and attacked – along the way!

Then, of course, there was the fact that the Russians had mistaken the British fishing fleet for Japanese warships. Although the actual attack had been at night, they'd

* A man named Hekkleman

passed them earlier that day in broad daylight and could clearly see that they were trawlers. The fishermen had even WAVED at them! But the Russian court concluded that it really had been a case of mistaken identity, with tragic consequences.

Imperial Russia finally accepted full responsibility for the fatal blunder and agreed that the naval officers would be put on trial in an international court.*

* When the Russian fleet arrived in the Far East they were attacked by the Japanese navy and badly defeated. So strong was anti-Russian feeling after the Dogger Bank incident that Britain awarded Japan's commander-in-chief, Admiral Togo, Britain's Order of Merit!

Horseplay

During the reign of Queen Victoria there was
a renewed interest in knights, chivalry and the
Middle Ages, affecting everything from books
to architecture to paintings. Scotsman Lord
Eglinton* decided to go one better by staging
his very own jousting tournament in 1839
at his private racecourse. The result was one
disaster after another.

* One of his famous ancestors had accidentally killed
the king of France in a real tournament back in 1559!

He allowed for a crowd of under 2,000, but when the day came over 100,000 people turned up. Eglinton hadn't taken the recently opened rail service from Euston Station in London into consideration!

Then the heavens opened, with rain pouring into the royal box. Nothing had been designed with bad weather in mind, and the open stands – and the costumes of many of those in them – were ruined. The rain was so bad that those playing the parts of the knights in armour couldn't see each other so had to abandon their sport. Then a nearby river began to flood the course.

There was a boar's head banquet and costume ball arranged for the evening which at least some of the visitors might have enjoyed, if it weren't for the fact that this was to have taken place in a tent . . . a tent that had ripped apart.

People fled back to the railway station in such numbers that many were left clinging to the outside of the train as it made its rain-soaked journey back to London.

Just not true!

Flying lizards can't fly – not because they don't have an airline ticket or boarding pass but because they don't have wings. Flying squirrels can't fly either. They are both excellent gliders, though. Both animals have large membranes of skin, like big flaps or sails, which let them glide through the air when they leap downwards.*

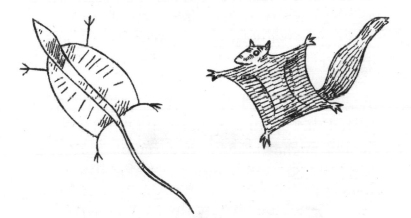

* Flying fish are also non-fliers, but they can leap out of the sea and high above the surface

A plan that bombed

A bungled attempt to assassinate Emperor
Napoleon III of France and his wife the
Empress Eugenie not only failed but actually
made the empress more popular. A bomb was
thrown at the imperial pair as they headed
for the opera, killing a number of people and
injuring many. Despite cuts, bruises and torn
clothing, Empress Eugenie famously told
officials not to worry about her husband and
her, because 'such risks are a part of our job'.
She instructed them to look after the wounded
instead.*

Eugenie, a Spanish 'commoner' by birth, had
already set up an orphanage in France with
money intended for her to spend on expensive
jewellery. She was a bit of a fashion icon too.**

In 1870, not long before the siege of Paris,***
Empress Eugenie was smuggled out of the

* Not only that, she later pleaded that the lives of her
would-be assassins should be spared
** The Princess Diana of her day
*** During which people became so short of food they
ended up eating cats and dogs

city to England by her American dentist! She eventually returned to Spain, where she died aged 93.

A terrible mess

Kings and queens throughout the centuries have made some sensational blunders and, because of who they are, these have been carefully recorded in the annals of history (for us to marvel at today), but few of them have been responsible for losing their country's Crown jewels.

King John* managed to lose England's Crown jewels IN THE WASH. (Pause for old joke.) No, he didn't forget to take them out of the pocket of his jeans before putting them in the washing machine.** The Wash is a river. King John and his forces were crossing the Wash where it meets the River Welland in a particularly marshy area.

Wagons laden with supplies, huge weapons, frightened horses and even the knights themselves in heavy armour found themselves sinking in the mud and quicksand. It was a

* Ruled 1199–1216
** Not only would they have had to be VERY BIG pockets, but denim – from which jeans are made – wasn't invented until the 19th century, and don't get me started about washing machines!

disaster. And among all these were the Crown jewels themselves, including the crown first worn by Edward the Confessor.*

After these terrible events, King John arrived at Swinburne Abbey, where he was offered food and drink. He could see that he'd upset the monks so, when he was offered cider, he insisted that the one who'd served him should drink some from the cup first. Without flinching the monk did this, so King John happily drank. He was unaware that the monk – who had indeed poisoned the wine – had now gone off somewhere else to die!

King John made it as far as Newark, where he died at the Bishop of Lincoln's castle on 19 October 1216.

The missing Crown jewels have yet to be found.

* Who, according to one children's history, 'slept under the dresser', but it only said that because it rhymed, not because there was any truth in it!

What a sparkler!

The most famous diamond in the world is probably the Koh-i-noor (Mountain Light), now set in the crown worn by King George VI's queen* at his coronation in 1937. It originally came into British hands when Britain annexed the Punjab in 1849.

The diamond was placed in the care of Sir John Lawrence, Governor of India, who promptly mislaid it. Three times letters came from England asking for it, each more desperate than the last. The third was from the Prime Minister himself. Sir John finally had his servants search high and low. Fortunately, one eventually found the diamond in a battered old tin box in Sir John's tool shed . . . in time for it to be sent to England to go on display in pride of place at the Great Exhibition in 1861.**

The diamond is large, but it used to be a

* Then known as Queen Elizabeth, but later known as 'Queen Elizabeth, the Queen Mother', being the mother of Queen Elizabeth II
** In the Crystal Palace in Hyde Park, London

whole lot bigger. When it was discovered, it is believed to have weighed a staggering 800 carats.* By the time it had been cut and come into Queen Victoria's possession it weighed just 191 carats (because whoever had cut it had bungled the job).

Amazingly, Victoria had it cut again, just so she could wear it as a brooch, and AGAIN the task wasn't carried out by the most skilled cutter around, reducing it to 108 carats, almost eight times lighter than it started out.**

Fortunately for those who care about such things, despite these blunders, its value remains at the 'priceless' end of expensive. It is on display with the other Crown jewels at the Tower of London. The last time that it was removed for a state occasion was following the death of Queen Elizabeth, the Queen Mother, when it was placed on her coffin and taken to Westminster Hall where she lay in state before her funeral in 2002.

* In 1913, a carat was fixed at 200 milligrams
** But still big by diamond standards

Cheesy?

The moon is not, in fact, made of cheese. This was proved once and for all as a result of the first moon landing, in 1969. The dimpled cheesy look (when viewed from Earth) is a result of the surface of the moon being pitted with craters, created by thousands of objects crashing into it over millions of years. Reports that numbers of mice have built rocket ships in order to try to reach what they believe to be a large round cheese hanging in the sky are also untrue. These are characters in works of fiction, usually intended for children. Mice do not have opposable thumbs so lack the ability to use tools to build and operate such vehicles.*

* They also lack the know-how**
** And probably don't think the moon looks anything like cheese anyway***
*** AND cheese is far from being a mouse's favourite food anyhow. That's just a myth

Flushed with excitement

When one of Napoleon's brothers, Louis, made himself ruler of the Netherlands, he decided he wanted a palace and chose Amsterdam town hall. It was certainly an impressive building, but there were two immediate problems. Firstly, new offices would have to be found for all the council workers* . . . and, secondly, the place had no running water. There wasn't a bathroom in the place.**

* Which probably didn't concern him too much
** Which may have been more of a bother

Blotting his copybook

Lewis Waterman was an insurance salesman who, in 1844, lost a contract – and the money he would have earned from it – when trying to sign the document. His quill pen splattered ink all over the wording. By the time he'd fetched a new document for signing, the potential client had done business with someone else.

This unfortunate mishap led to Waterman inventing the fountain pen, and one make of these pens still bears his name.

A touch of madness

When – or that should probably be 'if' – you compile a list of people you're going to have killed, it's probably best not to leave it lying about when you're sleeping, but that's exactly what the Emperor Commodus did. Then again, he'd gone a bit potty by then. The Romans began to realize that things weren't quite right when he declared that he was going to be a gladiator in the arena of the Colosseum* and that his gladiatorial name was to be Hercules . . . as in the god.**

Though he later changed his fighting name to Paulus, he still dressed like Hercules of legend, wandering around Rome dressed in a lion's skin and brandishing a club! He greatly enjoyed drinking too much and spending his time with actors and dancers – seen as a very unsavoury bunch – and was blissfully unaware of the high taxes others were imposing on citizens in his name.

* Speciality, throwing spears at lions
** The son of Zeus and that!

Then one night Commodus went to sleep, having drawn up that death list on a wax tablet. A servant boy found it and showed it to some of the people whose names appeared on it. Shortly after that, two of those named* provided their emperor with a bowl of poisoned wine. Now it was their turn to make a mess of things. Commodus wouldn't die. In the end they had to call in a wrestler who, in return for an enormous bribe,

strangled their victim. Not a happy tale.

---

* Laetus and Eclectus

Making a splash

The first person to successfully swim across the English Channel was Englishman Matthew Webb in 1875.* A woman didn't successfully swim across the Channel until 1926, when nineteen-year-old American Gertrude Ederle managed it in record time.** There were further celebrations when Dr Dorothy Logan was awarded a prize of £1,000 for her crossing, also in 1926 . . .

. . . which was a mistake. She'd cheated. Faked it. Fudged it in order to get the prize money. Eventually she ended up in court and was fined for gaining money under false pretences.

After this, crossings were more closely monitored and supervised.***

* In 21 hours, 45 minutes
** 14 hours, 39 minutes
*** The first person to swim the Channel in both directions was Englishman Edward Temme, but with a gap of several years in between! (France to England in 1927, then returning in 1934)****
**** The first person to swim it there and back nonstop was Antonio Abertondo in 1961*****
***** The first person to complete a three-way swim across the Channel was American Jon Erikson in 1981******
****** I think that's enough footnotes for now

Secrets from the dead

During the Second World War, German High Command knew that Allied forces were planning to attack Sardinia. The reason for their confidence was papers found in the possession of drowned Royal Marine Major William Martin, whose body had been washed up on a Spanish beach.

Along with the major's identity card, a photograph of his 'girl', a receipt for an engagement ring and a letter from Lloyds Bank saying that he must pay off his overdraft, was a letter. This letter was from the Vice Chief of the Imperial General Staff to General Alexander,* which made clear that the Allies were planning an attack in the western Mediterranean.

There was also a communiqué from Lord Louis Mountbatten to the Admiral of the Fleet and Commander in Chief, Mediterranean, to which Mountbatten had added a handwritten note, including the lines:

'Let me have him back as soon as the

---

* Then commanding the 18th Army Group in Africa

assault is over. He might bring home some sardines with him . . .'

Used to the British and their strange humour, German Intelligence took the mention of sardines – the fish – to be a reference to where the assault would take place: Sardinia.

So Field Marshal Wilhelm Keitel signed an order from Germany's Supreme Command of the Armed Forces sending troops to strengthen numbers in Sardinia.

He was blissfully unaware that this was EXACTLY what the British and their allies wanted Germany to do.

There was no planned attack on Sardinia. There wasn't even a Major William Martin. Every single one of the papers on his body was a forgery, from the letter from the bank to the receipt for the engagement ring.*

The body washed ashore wasn't of a drowned man. Yes, his lungs were filled with liquid, but that was because he had died of pneumonia. It

* Though Lord Mountbatten had genuinely handwritten the note

was enough to fool those carrying out a post mortem, who would have expected him to have died from drowning, given the circumstances.

In fact, his body had been placed in a canister packed with dry ice and put aboard the submarine *Seraph*, where it was taken to the waters outside the port of Huelva in south-west Spain. It was removed from the canister, placed in a life jacket and – after a brief burial service* – slipped into the water.

After this, everything went to plan. When the Allies attacked their real target – Sicily, not Sardinia – they faced far less resistance than they would have otherwise, many of the German forces now being in the wrong place at the wrong time.

The only piece of the jigsaw missing is the true identity of the made-up Major Martin. This remains an official secret to this day. His body was used for this extraordinary – and extraordinarily important – mission on the condition that it would never be revealed. He is buried in a graveyard in Huelva.

* Using the words of the service for a burial at sea

An explosive finish

In 2004, a sperm whale was washed up on a beach in Taiwan and died before it could be rescued. Scientists decided that the 17-metre, 50-ton carcass should be taken to a research centre for investigation, and it was loaded on to the back of a flatbed lorry.* As it was being driven through the middle of the town of Tainan, it exploded with the force of 30 grenades, splattering blood, guts and blubber all over the surrounding area. Amazingly, no one was killed or injured. This extraordinary turn of events was put down to a build-up of gases inside the body.

* A feat which took 13 hours, three large lifting cranes and 50 people!

Loser!

The composer Felix Mendelssohn composed some incidental music to be performed to the Shakespeare play *A Midsummer Night's Dream* ... then promptly lost the whole score!*

* To his credit, Mendelssohn got around this dreadful blunder by sitting down and writing it all again from memory**

** Lawrence of Arabia suffered a similar problem. He lost a big chunk of his autobiography, *The Seven Pillars of Wisdom*, and had to rewrite it

A fatal mistake

General Stonewall Jackson* was accidentally killed by his own men. A Confederate commander in the American Civil War, he decided to pay a surprise inspection to his front-line outposts.** It was night-time and, because it was dark and his visit unannounced, it was hardly surprising that he and his staff officers were mistaken for a sneaky enemy night attack. He was shot and wounded, dying a few days later.

* He got the nickname 'Stonewall' for standing firm against the enemy like a stone wall.
** During the battle of Chancellorsville in May 1863

All creatures great in plaster

The BBC TV series *All Creatures Great and Small*, starring Christopher Timothy* as vet James Herriot, ran for 90 episodes*** between 1978 and 1990 and was one of the corporation's biggest hits. Unfortunately, Timothy broke a leg in a car crash midway through the recording of the second series. Because the break couldn't be written into the storyline, they had to film 'around' it, avoiding showing Christopher Timothy's character walking anywhere very much, with more close-ups than usual and his sitting down rather a lot!

* Who went on to star in the daytime drama *Doctors*. James Herriot had previously appeared on the big screen, played by Simon Ward** in 1974 and then John Alderton in 1976
** Who played Winston Churchill in the film *Young Winston*. Robert Hardy, who played Siegfried Farnon, the head of Herriot's surgery, also played Churchill, in his case in *Winston Churchill: The Wilderness Years*
*** 87 standard 50-minute episodes and three 90-minute 'specials'

A weird beard situation

A series of commemorative stamps issued
in the US in 1893 – as part of the 400th
anniversary of Columbus's discovery of
the 'New World' for the west – is best
remembered for the impossibly fast-growing
beard!

The one-cent blue depicts 'Columbus in sight
of land' and there isn't so much as a hair on
his chinny-chin-chin. The two-cent purple
shows the actual landing. Although this
only occurred the day after land was sighted,
Christopher Columbus is now shown sporting

a rather fine beard. He may well have been a manly man, but it can't have grown THAT quickly!

In 1903, the island of St Kitts* issued their own inaccurate stamp commemorating Columbus. Like the US one-cent blue, their halfpenny purple-and-green showed the explorer sighting land. In this instance, he's depicted looking at it through a telescope . . . even though he never used such an instrument. How can we be so sure? Because the first practical telescope wasn't invented until over a hundred years after Columbus was dead and buried!

* In the West Indies

Not with a bang but a whimper

After much excitement and anticipation around the world, CERN's Large Hadron Collider* – the world's largest atom-smasher – was switched on, on 10 September 2008.

This moment was the culmination of 20 years' work at a cost of $5.46 billion, with a 16.9-mile machine containing 10,000 connections.** Some scientists were far from happy about the switch-on, seriously concerned that there was a genuine possibility that it could blow up the planet.

It broke down.

* CERN is the European Organization for Nuclear Research. A Large Hadron Collider is an enormous particle accelerator
** Such as how particles acquire their mass, and what happened during the 'Big Bang' that created the Universe

A right beating

Sir Jimmy Martin, inventor of the ejector seat,* made the mistake of intervening in a fight taking place near his home. The protagonists stopped fighting each other and turned on him instead. Sir Jimmy – whose invention has saved the lives of countless thousands of pilots in both peacetime and war – was so badly beaten that he required a metal plate in his head.

When he saw the plate provided by the hospital, Sir Jimmy instructed his own panel-beaters at his Martin-Baker** factory to make him a better one, which they did!

* Designing an ejector seat – more properly called an ejection seat – wasn't just about firing the pilot's chair free of the aircraft. A way had to be found to release the canopy above the pilot's head in the cockpit . . . and to get the pilot safely down to ground after ejection

** The Baker in Martin-Baker was James Martin's friend and colleague Valentine Baker, who was tragically killed when test-piloting one of their prototype planes

That sinking feeling again!

For his multi-Oscar-winning film *Titanic*, director James Cameron built an almost full-size replica of the starboard* side of the ship for the exterior scenes. Because some scenes took place on the opposite – port – side he used a film trick called 'flipping' where, when it's printed, the film is flipped to a mirror image so everything comes out back to front.

So that it didn't look like a reflection, all the writing on the ship (White Star Line logo, etc. and – in the dockside scene in Southampton – signs on passing vehicles) was put on back to front. This way, when the film was flipped all the writing looked the right way round.

The only problem with this ingenious money-saving idea is that the portside of the actual *Titanic* wasn't actually a mirror image of the starboard side.

* Starboard is the side of the ship facing right when it's moving forward. (The port side is the side facing left)

Whereas on the starboard side of the forward boat deck there were entrances to the first class gym and forward Grand Staircase, on the port side there was the entrance to the wireless room and windows to the officers' quarters. In Cameron's version you get to see the gym, etc. on both sides of the ship.*

* Not that most of us were aware of these errors, let alone spotted them!

'And the winner isn't . . .'

The People's Choice Award in the 2005 British Comedy Awards, which – as the name suggests – was decided by public vote, was given to comedy duo Ant and Dec* . . .

. . . even though the real winner was comedian and actress Catherine Tate, who later became even more widely known for her role in *Doctor Who* alongside David Tennant.

When this fix came to light in 2008, it seems that there were attempts to shift at least part of the blame on to rock star Robbie Williams who, it was claimed, had only agreed to hand out an award if it could be to Ant and Dec! Neither he nor Ant and Dec – who had legitimately won the award a number of times on previous occasions – had any idea what had happened.

The giving out of the award to someone other than the winner had not been an accident. The extraordinary blunder the organizers made was thinking that they could get away with it!

* Anthony McPartlin and Declan Donnelly

A bad egg

One of the most misused phrases used by people who like using such phrases is 'it's like the curate's egg', when something is thought to be all right in parts. The phrase refers to a cartoon* which appeared in the magazine *Punch* in 1895. It shows two men – the curate and his host – seated around a table having the following conversation:

> HOST: I'm afraid you've got a bad Egg, Mr. Jones!
>
> CURATE: Oh no, my Lord, I assure you! Parts of it . . . are excellent!

In other words, the egg has gone bad but, out of politeness,** the curate is quick to assure his host that it's fine in parts. The joke is, of course, that an egg which isn't entirely OK shouldn't be served up at all.

People, however, often take the phrase literally and use it to mean that something isn't all bad – entirely missing the point of the original joke!

* By George du Maurier
** Or timidity

Keep your eyes pealed!

Its a proofreader's job to spot misteaks in written text such as this. He or she has to look out for typin errors, grammatical errors, spellling mistakes, factual errors and and any thing else that isnt write.Their are 15 deliberate errors on this page Can you spot them all? The answers are on page 294.

- The word should be peeled (as in skinned) in the heading, not pealed (as in rung like a bell)
- Its should read It's
- misteaks should be mistakes
- typin should be typing
- spellling should have two 'l's, not three!
- There should only be one and immediately after 'factual errors',
- any thing should be one word: anything
- isnt should be isn't
- write should be right
- There should be a space between the full stop and the word Their
- And anyway, Their should be There
- There are 14 deliberate mistakes, not 15
- A full stop is missing between 'page' and 'Can'.
- The answers aren't on page 294. (There isn't one.) They're here!

Leaving your mark

It is a mistake to state with absolute certainty that two fingerprints from different people will never be found to be the same. What one can say is that, based on all the evidence so far, it's highly unlikely. As Colin Beavan points out in his 2001 book *Fingerprints*, there is also no proof that everyone will die. But don't hold your breath waiting for someone to live forever.*

* It might kill you

Better in than out

In January 1992 President George Bush*
was sick into the lap of the Japanese prime
minister during a state dinner. The whole
embarrassing incident was captured on film!

* Father of President George W. Bush

How to lose friends and upset people

The Spanish basketball team at the 2008 Olympic Games in China was photographed for an advertisement, trying to make their eyes slant 'to look Chinese'. Following the resulting outrage, one of the players* tried to defend their actions by saying that the team had thought that it would have be seen as 'an affectionate gesture'! Wrong.

* Point guard José Manuel Calderón

Well red

Most of us are only too well aware that the tomato is actually a fruit and not a vegetable. It's one of those did-you-know? facts to which over 90 per cent of people yawn and reply, 'Well, yes, I did know, thank you very much!'* It has been pointed out, however:

'Knowledge is knowing that tomato is a fruit. Wisdom is not putting one in a fruit salad.'**

* Or something far more rude
** By the late*** columnist, humourist, and writer Miles Kingston, who came up with it first
*** As in 'no longer living'

The meaning of love

One of the most famous lines – and central themes – of the 1970 tear-jerker film *Love Story* is spoken by the character played by Ryan O'Neal. It is:

'Love means never having to say you're sorry.'

This has puzzled many a film-goer who knows only too well that loves means being able to say you're sorry. And being forgiven.

In the 1972 film *What's Up, Doc?* Barbra Streisand's character says the very same line to the selfsame Ryan O'Neal, who responds with:

'That's the dumbest thing I ever heard . . .'

Now *that's* a good line!

Double trouble?

In the Australian TV soap *Home and Away*, there used to be twins Jade and Kirsty Sutherland played by Kate Garven and Christie Hayes. Being twins, they had an amazing telepathic empathy so one would know when the other was in trouble: something which happened often enough in the storylines over the years. Imagine the viewers' surprise, then, when it finally transpired that there'd been a mix-up in the hospital at birth and that they WEREN'T twins after all. Ooops! All mention of the telepathic empathy was conveniently forgotten.

NOTE: For a short time Kirsty and Laura, the 'real' Sutherland twins who turned out to be identical – were both played by Hayes. All the characters eventually left, with Kirsty (now Kirsty Phillips) returning to fictional Summer Bay in 2008.

We think ice is rather nice

On 18 October 1867, the Russians sold Alaska to the US for a staggering $7.2 million, which was a mind-blowingly GINORMOUS sum of money back then. Little wonder that the deal quickly became known as Steward's Folly after the US Secretary of State who'd gone with the deal. What use was a vast expanse of icy nothingness?

What seemed like a ridiculous blunder on the part of the US was later seen in a very different light when oil was discovered under Alaska . . . so much that when it came to compensating the relatives of those living in Alaska at the time it was purchased, the US government could easily afford to pay them $963 million (along with 44 million acres of land)!

242

Boom! Boom!

The storming of the Winter Palace* was the climax of the Russian Revolution, when the Bolsheviks planned to lay siege to the building that housed the provisional government, now that Tsar Nicholas II had abdicated. Thousands of Russian workers gathered outside the Winter Palace and the cruiser *Aurora* – crewed by communist revolutionaries – opened fire on it.

Despite the loud 'BOOM!' there was no shattering of glass or crumbling of masonry. They hadn't wanted to damage the building, so fired blanks! It did act as a signal for the men to storm the palace, rifles at the ready, which they did . . . only to find the front door unlocked and the building empty.

The provisional government was long gone. The Bolsheviks could simply have walked up to the front door unarmed and taken a casual stroll inside!

* On 25 October 1917 (by the Russian calendar)

Don't be fooled

A koala is not a bear and a Giant Panda was
thought not to be a bear but turns
out to be one after all. A red
panda, however, is more
closely related to a raccoon. A
spider monkey isn't a spider but a
monkey – but you already knew
that – and a starfish
isn't a fish, which is
why they're more properly
known as sea
stars. Although
beaver-skin
hats really
are made of
beaver-skin,
catgut is
actually sheep's
gut. Seahorses
aren't
horses, and
glow-worms aren't worms but
insects. A ladybird isn't a bird
but a bug, which probably explains

why they're called ladybugs in the US. As for coffee beans, they're not really beans, but you'll have to take my word for it.*

* I need a little lie-down

A stack of Bibles

As the bestselling book of all time, it's hardly surprising that the Bible has had its fair share of misprints. Unfortunately, many of them have appeared in the most inappropriate places. Here's a list of just some of them:*

 The Ears to Ear Bible – so called because this 1810 edition contains the misprint 'Who hath ears to *ear*, let him hear' (instead of 'Who hath ears to hear . . .') in Matthew 13:43.

 The Forgotten Sins Bible (of 1638) in which Luke 7:47, 'Her sins which are many, are forgiven', reads: 'Her sins which are many, are *forgotten*'.

 The Judas Bible (of 1611) in which Judas Iscariot's name appears in Matthew 26:36, instead of Jesus's!!!

 The Lions Bible (of 1804) which contained an enormous number of printers' errors including, most famously, 'but thy son that

---

* Which also appears in *Philip Ardagh's Book of Absolutely Useless Lists for Absolutely Every Day of the Year*

shall come forth out of thy *lions'* instead of 'out of thy loins', hence its name.

 The Printers' Bible (of c.1702) in which in Psalms 119:161, 'princes have persecuted me without cause', appears as '*printers* have persecuted me without cause' . . . due to a printer's error!

 The Sin On Bible (of 1716) is probably the most famous of the misprinted Bibles. John 5:14 should read 'sin no more', but appears as 'sin *on* more', meaning quite the opposite!

 The To-Remain Bible (of 1805) is particularly interesting because an editor's comment written in the margin of the proof pages – pages which are corrected before the final printing – ended up in the final bound Bible. Galatians 4:29 should read: 'persecuted him that was born after the spirit, even so it is now'. It appeared as: 'persecuted him that was born after the spirit *to remain*, even so it is now'. The words 'to remain' were a note from an editor that the comma after the word spirit was to remain. The printer thought it meant that he should add the words to the text!

 The Unrighteous Bible (of 1653) also contains a serious altering of meaning. Instead of I Corinthians 6:9 stating 'the unrighteous shall not inherit the Kingdom of God', it claims: 'the unrighteous *shall* inherit the Kingdom of God'!

 The Wicked Bible (of 1631) contains the unfortunate commandment: 'Thou shalt commit adultery.' The printers were fined £300 and went out of business.

Foam alone

It's a common misconception that the more suds – bubbles – a washing powder makes, the better it cleans. This just ain't so, but the manufacturers didn't use to mind people believing that because it was easy enough to create suds. In fact, some of the early synthetic detergents were made to produce so many suds that they clogged drains and sewers. Not only that – once in lakes and streams, the thick film of suds on the surface stopped air getting into the water. The result? Plants and animals dying.

Alternating between genius and something else

Nikola Tesla was an extraordinary man. Late in life, he bought new gloves every week, only used hankies once, wiped his plates clean with a napkin before eating off them, used clean towels every time he washed and tried not to shake hands with anyone – ever – unless it was absolutely necessary. But he loved pigeons, which have a reputation for being dirty and are referred to by some people as 'flying rats'. The birds would often follow him into hotels, restaurants and libraries, much to other people's disgust and outrage!*

But who was this man? Despite his eccentricities,** the naturalized American (born Croatian) was a brilliant scientist who actually turned down a Nobel Prize. He proved that by using an alternating current, electricity could

---

* Hang on a minute! With all that pigeon poo around, maybe all that obsessive cleaning made absolute sense?

** Or, perhaps, because of them

travel miles away from the power station where it was generated, to light and heat people's homes.* The world-famous inventor Thomas Edison used a direct current, which could only travel short distances. Tesla's is the method we still use today, but he didn't bother to patent any of his ideas, so it was other people who grew rich from them.

Tesla invented a whole host of things, from the neon tube – used for all those weirdly lit signs – to a way of relieving pain using electricity. At one stage he had a 60-metre-high mast with a copper ball on top with which he created incredible storms of thunder and lightning!

He once claimed to have built a 'telegeodynamic oscillator' in his New York laboratory: a death-ray machine powerful enough to reduce the Empire State Building to a heap of rubble in a few minutes. He had, he said, destroyed the device because he didn't want it falling into the wrong 👉

* An alternating current flows in one direction then the other and so on and so on, 100 times a second. It travels long distances with very little loss of power

hands. His idea was that a death beam could surround a country 'like an invisible Chinese wall',* making it impregnable against attack, therefore making war impossible ... So it was intended as a peaceful death ray then!

Was this the fantasy of an eccentric or a statement of fact from a brilliant scientist? We'll never know. When he died, he left

* He must have been thinking of the Great Wall of China

few scientific papers.*

Tesla had once stated that he would live to be 150. He actually died in 1943, aged an impressive 86, so we know that he wasn't always right about everything.

A not-so-secret agent

Mata Hari is probably one of the most famous female spies of all time, which is a bit surprising when you consider that she was rubbish at it. Her real name was Margaretha Geertruida Zelle and she was Dutch . . . though on stage she called herself Mata Hari, the Oriental Dancing Star' with a Javanese prince for a father.* In the First World War she became a German spy but, having a larger-than-life personality, soon attracted the attention of the Allied counter-intelligence. When they went to boot her out of France, where she was living at the time, she offered to spy for them instead.

Amazingly, they gave her the name of some Belgian secret agents to contact, one of whom was promptly arrested by the Germans and executed. This suggested that she wasn't the most trustworthy of people. Soon neither the Germans nor the Allies wanted her working for them.

* Mata Hari means 'Eye of the Dawn'

After a bit of skulduggery, where the Germans appear to have mentioned her in a message written in a code which they knew the Allies had cracked and would be able to decode, Mata Hari was arrested and brought to trial by the Allies in July 1917. She was executed on 15 October 1917.

So why is she remembered as being such a great spy? Because the French authorities used her to their advantage. With fighting conditions so appalling and the war seeming to go badly for the Allies, a number of French regiments mutinied and had to be suppressed.

As part of a cover-up, the French authorities claimed that their troops had been betrayed and – conveniently – Mata Hari had been behind it. Soon stories grew up that she alone had been responsible for the deaths of over 50,000 French soldiers.

Lies, all lies!

It's a lie to say that a lie detector can tell whether someone is lying or not, which is why the results of lie-detector tests are inadmissable in courts in the UK and the US. Detectors monitor heart rate, blood pressure, breathing and sweating and, in addition, the skilled operator watches the subject for other telltale signs of whoppers being told. All the most skilled lie-detector operator can do is give a professional estimate of the percentage of likelihood as to whether someone is lying or not. It is not an exact science. With practice, some people can 'beat' the lie detector, 'fooling' the machine.

Best foot forward

Birds' knees don't bend backwards (compared to our human knees). It's a common mistake to think that. It's not that your eyes are deceiving you. It's just that what we think of as being their knees are their ankles and what we think of as their feet are their toes! Here's a diagram to make it absolutely clear:

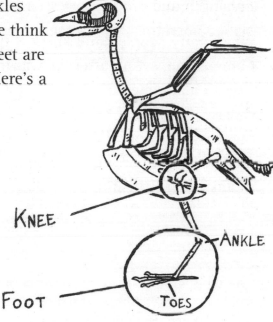

KNEE

ANKLE

FOOT

TOES

The filthy truth

Florence Nightingale* – the Lady with the Lamp – is remembered for her tireless work trying to make conditions better for injured and dying British soldiers during the Crimean War, and for her major role in helping to turn nursing into a proper profession.

What many people don't know is that a Royal Commission, set up after the war to discover why so many men died of sickness and disease, found that her hospital at Scutari was the worst offender. TWICE as many patients died because of a lack of hygiene there than in any other British military hospital!**

* An unusual woman, for many years she kept a pet owl in her pocket. She went to bed in 1896 and stayed there until her death in 1910, using it as an office from which she wrote hundreds and hundreds of letters
** To be fair, Florence Nightingale hadn't built the hospital and she had done an enormous amount to try to improve conditions there. She didn't argue with the findings of the commission either. She understood the importance of hygiene and wanted people to learn from these mistakes

Just pretending

If you didn't want to upset the gods, then making Julius Caesar the chief priest of Rome – the Pontifex Maximus – probably wasn't the smartest move. He didn't believe in them! He thought that the Roman gods and goddesses were a bunch of made-up characters in a bunch of made-up stories! (Still, he wasn't bothered, because he didn't think they could strike him down with a thunderbolt if they didn't exist!*)

* The gods, that is. Not thunderbolts. Thunderbolts certainly exist

What a way to go

William the Conqueror is probably best remembered for winning the Battle of Hastings in 1066,* which didn't take place in Hastings but in a place (now) called Battle. What's less well remembered is how he was treated AFTER death.

When he died, in around 1087, everything in the room – including some of the clothes he'd been wearing – was stolen. He was to have a grand funeral at the church of St Stephen in Caen, France, but a fire broke out nearby. People who'd been lining the streets for the funeral procession dashed out to either (a) help put out the flames, or (b) watch other people put out the flames.

Once inside the church, the monks found William's body wouldn't fit in the stone coffin prepared for him. (No one had bothered to check first.) They tried pushing it in this way and that . . . and with such force that, in the end, his bowels burst. The church was filled

* Where his enemy, King Harold, didn't get an arrow in his eye

with such an unimaginably horrible stench
that the funeral service had to be rushed
through. But the indignity didn't end there . . .

Just under 500 years later, in 1562, William's
tomb was opened during a 'disturbance'
and the bones from his skeleton ended up
scattered all over the place. When it came to
putting them back, all that could be found
was a single thigh bone. This was reburied
with due pomp and ceremony during a special
service. But things didn't end there . . .

During the French Revolution – some 700
years after his death! – William the Conqueror
(or his thigh bone, at least) was seen as a
symbol of wealth and power . . . so his tomb
was destroyed!!!

Enough to puzzle a monkey

From July 1876 to March 1878, author and poet Thomas Hardy lived in a semi-detached house in Sturminster Newton, overlooking the River Stour.* It was here that he wrote his famous novel *The Return of the Native*. There's even a plaque on the front of the house to commemorate it, placed there in the 1990s . . . though, back in the 1980s, Professor Michael Millgate offered pretty conclusive proof that it's the WRONG house. According to him, they got the right building but the wrong half! The professor's evidence included a photograph of the Hardy Players outside the actual house in 1921 – the one without the plaque – and Hardy had been there with them . . . and he should know where he lived!

Part of the confusion may have arisen from a monkey-puzzle tree out front. It was known that Hardy had planted one in front of his

---

* There are lots of rivers called Stour in the UK because the word 'stour' actually means river . . . so, in one sense, this is the River River!

home and – sure enough – there one was (and later the remains of it) in front of the house where they put up the plaque. Professor Millgate asserts that Hardy had planted two trees, but the one outside next-door's house outlived his!

Paws for thought

Sir Isaac Newton may have invented the cat door*. He is supposed to have had one cut into the back door of his home, Woolsthorpe Manor. When he later acquired a kitten, he had a second, smaller opening added for it to use. It appears not to have occurred to him that it could have shared the bigger cat's door!**

* A cat flap without the flap part
** Though there are some (spoilsports) who claim that the scientist owned neither cat, kitten nor dog!

No stick-in-the-mud

As a young man, King Henry VIII was said to have been a dashing chap, rather than the overweight bearded person we often think of.* Having said that, he did spend a fair amount of time blundering about.

In 1524, during a friendly joust, he forgot to pull down the visor on the front of his helmet and, guess what, he got a piece of broken lance in his face.

In 1525, for some reason he decided to try pole-vaulting across a muddy ditch (when he was out hunting). The pole broke and he landed head first in the ditch, with such force that his head became firmly stuck in the mud.

His footman** managed to pull out the struggling royal, who was finding it hard to breathe.

---

* Unless you've been watching Jonathan Rhys Meyers playing him in the TV series *The Tudors*
** Grabbing him by the feet, one imagines

A right turkey!

In St Mary's Church at Lübeck in Germany there were some ancient wall paintings which had deteriorated over the centuries.In 1948, Professor Dietrich Fey was given the task of sensitively restoring them to their former glory. Unfortunately, he seriously botched the job and ended up destroying them. The walls were left bare!

Embarrassing though this was, it would probably have been best for the professor if he'd admitted his terrible mistake and moved on. Instead he had the brilliantly misguided idea of hiring an artist to paint some new pictures.

Incredibly, he didn't even ask the artist – Lothar Malskat – to try to make them look like the original frescoes. He let him paint what he liked so long as the pictures looked in keeping and suitably old!

Using illustrations in an art-history book as a guide, Malskat painted away behind a screen for years (while everyone thought painstaking restoration was under way). In

1951, Professor Fey unveiled the fruits of 'his work'.

Art critics and historians alike were falling over themselves to praise these ancient paintings given new life thanks to the professor's undeniable expertise . . . but there were a few puzzling factors, the biggest being a turkey.

One of Malskat's much-admired pictures was of such a bird, but turkeys hadn't been introduced to Europe – from the New World – until hundreds of years after these pictures were supposedly painted!

Meanwhile, Professor Fey and Herr Malskat fell out over something or other, and Malskat broke his silence, announcing that he had painted the fresco. Amazingly, people seemed reluctant to believe him at first . . . until he produced photographs of the blank walls after Fey's accident!

Only then did the so-called experts notice that the paints used were modern, as was the plaster under them! Not only that – and no chuckling, please – the faces of the saints included one of German film star Marlene Dietrich!!!*

Both Fey and Malskat ended up in prison and the walls in St Mary's Church, Lübeck, were stripped bare. Incredibly though, this was not before two stamps had been issued in good faith showing images from the faked wall paintings!

* I love this detail!

The eyes have it

There are a number of legends surrounding the life – and death – of St Lucy. One version has it that, in the fourth century, when a nobleman proposed to her he made the mistake of using a chat-up line about wanting to marry her for her beautiful eyes.

She is said to have ripped out her eyeballs and handed them to him, saying, 'Now let me give myself to God.' Her would-be husband denounced her as a Christian to the authorities and she was martyred,* but not before her eyesight was miraculously restored through a fresh pair of eyes.

Happy now?

If you ever see a painting of a woman carrying spare eyes on a platter, you can be pretty sure that it's St Lucy.

* Attempts to move her and then burn her proved impossible, so she was stabbed to death on the spot

Strewth, mate!

The Sydney Harbour Bridge was officially opened at a ribbon-cutting ceremony on 19 March 1932. The ribbon was supposed to be cut by Australian premier Jack Lang. The mistake police made was not to pay close attention to a uniformed man on a horse nearby. Everyone simply assumed that he was part of the official opening ceremony.

In truth, Francis de Groot* was about to take matters into his own hands. As a protest, he galloped forward (on his borrowed horse) and slashed at the ribbon with a sword. It was captured on film and seen on newsreels in cinemas all over Australia . . . until the Australian government managed to get it banned.

A more recent mistake is the belief that before either de Groot or Jack Lang got near the ribbon it was actually cut by a mysterious woman. This misinformation came out of a mockumentary** made for fun in the 1990s!

* Who strongly believed that the ribbon should be cut by a member of the British royal family
** A mock documentary

A tuck in time

The legendary adventures of Robin Hood are set in the time of the reign of Richard the Lionheart (1189-1199), mostly when the king was abroad fighting the Crusades and his 'evil' brother, John, was ruling on his behalf. Friars didn't arrive in England until the early 13th century, however, so how Friar Tuck could have been one of Robin's Merry Men is a mystery. Or a mistake!*

* The earliest known mention of a friar in a Robin Hood story is in 'Robin Hood and the Curtal Friar', but he has no name. Friar Tuck is mentioned by name in a play from 1475. In the 1400s there was a real-life chaplain on the run called Robert Stafford who used the alias 'Friar Tuck'

Cuckoo! Cuckoo!

On April Fool's Day in 2008, Benjamin Jorgensen and Donna Hayes tried to hold up the Cuckoo Restaurant in Olinda, Australia. It was such a bungled attempt that the judge trying the case described the pair as 'the Keystone Robbers'.*

Jorgensen confronted the manager, Peter Schmidt, with a sawn-off shotgun as he was leaving the restaurant. When he demanded Schmidt hand over the bag he was carrying, the manager told him that there were only bread rolls in it. Jorgensen, however, was convinced that he was lying and that the bag contained around AU$30,000.

As he took the bag off Schmidt, Jorgensen accidentally shot his girlfriend accomplice, Hayes, in the hip. As she lay on the ground screaming, 'You got me! You got me!'

---

* The Keystone Cops were a bunch of bungling policemen – actors, not the real thing – in a series of American silent movies (of the same name) starting in 1912. Different actors played the cops in different films, but the characters were always totally incompetent!

Jorgensen took Schmidt's car keys and proceeded to try to use them on completely the wrong vehicle.

The bag had, indeed, only contained rolls and the bungling robbers were soon caught, with Jorgensen making a full confession. As well as pleading guilty to the armed robbery, he also pleaded guilty to 'negligently causing serious injury'. He claimed that he'd brought along the loaded weapon to scare people with the noise rather than hurt anyone.

Who do you do?

Pop star Christina Aguilera visited a computer exhibition in Las Vegas in 2003. While she was standing around looking at a computer, a man came up to her, introduced himself, and said that he'd be happy to show her anything, or answer any technical questions she might have. Nonplussed, and probably thinking that he was just another computer geek, Aguilera replied, 'Thanks, buddy, but I've already got a computer guy who can do that.' The man was the boss of Microsoft, Bill Gates.

On another occasion, Aguilera was introduced to probably the most famous golfer in the world, Tiger Woods, who told her that he had all her CDs.

'Sorry, I don't follow tennis,' said Aguilera, 'so I don't know much about you.'

Roddy Doyle Ha! Ha! Ha!

In July 2000, the *Observer* newspaper printed a correction following the publication of a recommended reading list from Roddy Doyle in an earlier special 'summer reading' feature in their 'Review' section. The list did, indeed, contain recommendations from Roddy Doyle . . .

. . . but not Roddy Doyle 'the celebrated Irish author'.* According to the correction, the Roddy Doyle who supplied them with 'a very interesting selection of summer reading' was a computer engineer from north London.

* Whose works include the children's book *The Giggler Treatment*

Wild goose chase?

Aristocratic French ladies with more time on their hands than was good for them decided to hold a race for their exotic and unusual pets in the grounds of the Sporting Society of Compiègne in 1901.* Things started interestingly when the animals were paraded on leads.** When the lion cub rolled over, it took its owner, the Princess de Lucinge, with it. She knocked into the Baroness de la Motte and her black goat, sending her sprawling . . . and their two pets ended up in a fight.

The actual race was soon under way and fraught with dangers. Most concern was for the Egyptian dung beetle belonging to Mademoiselle Fournier-Sarlovèze. There were fears that it might be eaten or trampled by another competitor. Then, when the insect veered off the racecourse into the long grass, the fear was that it might get lost! The

---

* The entrants were: a monkey, a goose, a bantam, a turkey, a tortoise, a duck, a black goat, a guinea hen, a sheep, an Egyptian dung beetle and a lion cub
** And brightly coloured ribbons

monkey,
meanwhile,
tried throttling a
fellow competitor,
the bantam, but –
eventually – crossed
the winning line first.

The race did not become an annual event.

Who checks the checkers?

In November 2008, the head of the UK's Security Industry Authority, responsible for vetting would-be security guards (to make sure that they were the right sort of people for the job) lost his job. The reason given was that it was because he hadn't vetted 38 people doing the vetting, to see whether THEY were the right sort of people to be doing THEIR jobs!

The authority's blunders included giving the Metropolitan Police the go-ahead to employ 12 security guards who turned out to be illegal immigrants and shouldn't have been in the country, let alone working . . . let alone for the police!

In his sights

Private Henry Tandey VC, DCM, MM was the most highly decorated private in the British army in the First World War. Just before the Second World War, British Prime Minister Neville Chamberlain visited Adolf Hitler in his new Bavarian retreat at Berchtesgaden, 2,000 metres up a mountain . . .

. . . and there on Hitler's wall was a copy of a famous painting of Tandey carrying a wounded comrade.

Hitler explained to the puzzled Prime Minister that Private Tandey had had the opportunity to shoot him – Adolf Hitler – as a young soldier but, seeing that he was unarmed at the time, had lowered his rifle and spared his life. He then went on to ask Chamberlain to pass on his best wishes to Tandey when he returned to England.*

If these events truly happened, some might argue that by making 'the mistake' of

* According to Tandey's family, Chamberlain did phone him

saving Hitler's life, millions had been condemned to death in a later war . . . but life doesn't work like that!*

* And some argue that the dates don't quite match up and that Hitler was either mistaken or myth-making. Either way, it makes a remarkable story

Recipe book

During a game of football in the early 1980s, Mike Bagley of Bristol was booked by the referee for use of bad language. Bagley was so ENRAGED by this that he snatched the ref's notebook, tore out the page on which his name had been entered, and ATE IT!

He was sent off.

And banned for six weeks.

In 1989, Fernando d'Ercoli (playing for Pianta against Arpax in Italy) went one better. When he was shown a red card by the ref, he ate the whole thing!

Did you spot?

Did you notice that the bee drawn on the blackboard in the picture on page 146 is not a bumblebee at all? It's a honey bee. Bumblebees are much more round and bumbly!

I did! I spotted it . . .

. . . just now.

Philip Ardagh